Tangela Johnson is a Seer ˻ this planet to make you comfortable; she's here to help you see who you're meant to be and strip away the limiting beliefs that keep you 'less than' your fullest expression and potential. Consider this book her Intervention, a gift to you in love.

— Stefanie Crowe,
Entrepreneur and Wealth Strategist

Meeting and working with Tangela helped solidify and give a name to a concept and a pattern I've lived out instinctively for decades. "Relaxed Power" is like a decoder ring for your own behavior, revealing subtle patterns that can inform the successes and failures, struggles and triumphs of life. If you're interested in coming to a better understanding of your own unique purpose and power—and who isn't?—read Tangela's book!

— Mark McKnight,
President/CEO, Reflection Riding

As an HR Executive, I've relied on Tangela for the past 10 years to help me and other professionals understand how to identify and channel who they truly are into a more powerful version of one's self. Her insights and ability to help individuals level up is unmatched!—Particularly for women who are often unfamiliar or uncomfortable harnessing their true power. She helps all of us, men and women, understand how to be great, but in a way that is authentic, evolved, unforced and yes—relaxed!

— Marie Webb,

Vice President of Human Resources,

Electric Power Board (EPB)

RELAXED POWER

TANGELA W. JOHNSON

13TH & JOAN

© 2019 by Tangela W. Johnson
Relaxed Power

Published by 13th & Joan

All rights reserved. No part of this publication may be reproduced, distributed, or transmitted in any form or by any means, including photocopying, recording, or other electronic or mechanical methods, without the prior written permission of the publisher, except in the case of brief quotations embodied in critical reviews and certain other noncommercial uses permitted by copyright law. For permission requests, write to the publisher, addressed "Attention: Permissions Coordinator," at the address below.

13th & Joan
500 N. Michigan Avenue, Suite #600
Chicago, IL 60611
WWW.13THANDJOAN.COM

Ordering Information:
13th & Joan books may be purchased for educational, business or sales promotional use. For information, please email the Sales Department at sales@13thandjoan.com.

Printed in the United States of America

ISBN: 978-1-7342346-2-6

Publisher's Cataloging-in-Publication data has been applied for.

First Edition Printed, 2019
Library of Congress Cataloging-in-Publication Data
has been applied for.

First Edition
10 9 8 7 6 5 4 3 2 1

Dedicated to Aunt Shirley and My Amazing Parents.

TABLE OF CONTENTS

PREFACE

I TOLD MY DAUGHTER THAT SHE SHOULD make people laugh at my funeral. She could start by telling them what an average-to-bad cook I am. She claims that I have discovered ten ways to bake chicken, and all of them are very average to very bad. In addition to making people laugh, I told her to make mine a short funeral service because it's useless to try to say in one or two hours what should have been spoken over a lifetime.

Death is one of our greatest fears, but I think we often fear living as much as we fear death. For whatever reasons, I have a greater fear of living a mundane, "settle for" life than I have of dying. I've always been more interested in discovering the role I'm supposed to play in this finite moment in eternity. Understanding that death is certain, but living is a choice, has simplified things for me. When I was a kid, we would draw these Kilroy cartoon figures of a balding man with a long nose peeking over a wall. We would draw it everywhere to announce that we existed, that we mattered, and that we had made a mark on that place. All of us need our, "Wuz Here" self-portrait.

On some level, even as a young child, I've always pondered my own existence. I think it's Reverend Curtis Johnson's doing. Growing up in the rural South, in a small Baptist church, I remember many Sundays when Rev. Johnson would end his sermon with the following: "I look forward to the day when I stand before God, and He says to me, 'Well done, thy good and faithful servant. Well done.'" His booming voice would rise to a fever pitch when he quoted this scripture from Matthew 25:23. His passionate connection to those words caused me to ponder even deeper the meaning of my own life and what my assignment on the earth would be. The impact of his words never left my spirit. Those powerful words became my living mantra and fueled my desire to become a student of me, so I can fully embrace every day with excitement and expectation.

William Barclay, the controversial and brilliant twentieth century University of Glasgow professor said, "There are two great days in a person's life—the day we are born and the day we discover why." This powerful statement can be attributed to each human being. Discovering one's inner greatness and purpose is an arduous journey. The first step is seeking, but we often don't even know where to start. Many people doubt that it is possible to live a called life. They believe it is for the rich, the famous, the musicians, the internet start-up mavericks, and the lucky ones who were just born understanding their greatness. Nothing could be further from the truth. Those you see in the limelight may have instinctively labored to pursue their dream where you have not. However, even those seemingly "gifted" people may not understand their calling or purpose. We'll discuss the distinction between your gift and your calling later in this book.

All of us are powerful; we simply don't know it yet. We have to be open to understanding what fuels our joy as well as what hinders us from living our best life. We are one piece of wisdom away from being our most powerful self. Throughout my life, I've asked the God of the universe to reveal to me the important things I need to know about myself. Admittedly, some of those revelations have been painful to accept and even more painful to change. As daunting as it is, we all have to transform ourselves to become our greatest and most powerful selves. More often than not, that transformation requires vulnerability and hard self-truths, both of which challenge us spiritually and emotionally.

A wonderful Uber driver and I had a delightful conversation as he drove me the thirty minutes to the airport. He was a retired ski instructor, and it was obvious that he understood the human psyche more than most. All those years of teaching people how to effectively get on two flat metal sticks and zoom down a mountain would require you to understand people! He and I talked about politics and business and really had a great discussion. Just as we were about to part ways, he gave me a great compliment which I shall never forget. He said that I have a "relaxed power." I replied with an awkward "thank you" but his words struck me so profoundly, I knew I would ponder them for weeks to come. It has never occurred to me to use the words "relaxed" and "power" together. He was able to synthesize, in two words, what I have been striving for my entire life: which is to be completely me. Relaxed power means that I live a purposed life, not a perfect life. Perfection is an illusion—a pressure cooker. Ultimately, "relaxed power" means that—on some level—I've learned to marry my inner divinity (my purpose) with my humanity (my imperfections) in ways that create spiritual and emotional harmony. That harmony allows me to give myself to others and to receive from them. Essentially, it means that I am comfortable in my complexities. I can simultaneously be resilient and weak—powerful and vulnerable. After half of a century, I've only scratched the surface of who I really am and my capacity to impact the world around me. Don't get me wrong, I am excited and grateful for the wisdom I've gained thus far, but there is more to know, to ponder, and to share with others. This book is about sharing wisdom with you, so you can walk in your own unique, relaxed power.

Greatness, purpose, and called living are there for your taking. Greatness comes in many forms; it has vast uses and many evolutions that can change your life and the world in significant ways. You can't live life on autopilot; nor can you go through the motions. You have to be willing to take the risks of knowing you better and holding yourself accountable for manifesting your own greatness. No one on earth can do it for you; therefore, no one on earth can take the blame or credit for your successes or failures.

Admittedly, over the years, my creative and entrepreneurial mind has concocted many ideas, most of which were marginal at best—or just outright bad. My multiple attempts to birth my "greatness" have given my life a deep sense of adventure and expectation. Somehow my crazy, winding path has infused wisdom, confidence, courage, joy, and a sense of well-being that I would not have otherwise experienced. My most successful ideas have had their own evolution of sorts. In 2011, while working earnestly on my talking points for a presentation I was making to a women's networking group, the title of my twenty-minute talk was "Courageous Leadership." Looking back on it, a more appropriate title would have been "Courageous Living." At that time, I honestly didn't feel that I had a strong sense of what the word "courageous" meant. People need well-defined concepts and proper context to fully understand a message. I needed a definition that could be expressed practically, simply, and profoundly, so I did the only thing I knew to do: I prayed for brilliance. My prayers were answered with the *Self-Transformation Model* that you'll read about in this book. This model evolved into my coaching model. The more I use it to help people self-discover, the more I become convinced that most of us are mired in a foggy emotional state that hinders us from living a vibrant life. Working with people has intensified my desire to dissect our life journey and examine why some of us thrive and live happy, productive lives and why others of us struggle to find our place in the world.

This book is a combination of my personal journey and my experience as an organizational development consultant and coach. My journey has been as a person who has sought to constantly nurture and develop the gifts and talents that support my purpose. Most of my mentors have been men, starting with my dad. He simultaneously nurtured and challenged me. A woman's confidence comes from her father. Our fathers or father-figures give us permission to embrace our greatness. My dad did that for me. Consequently, he positioned me to be comfortable asking for guidance and wisdom from multiple sources. It just so happened that the people who were doing what I wanted to do in business were men. Their gender, race, and nationality didn't matter to me. What mattered to me was gaining the wisdom that I needed to be effective. Frankly, I wanted to shape my own destiny and not have my life feel like a jolting, bumper car ride at a theme park. We need each other to be great; I discovered that principle through those willing souls who invested in me. I have made it a part of my lifestyle to pay it forward. Professionally, I have helped others self-discover and develop their individual greatness. On the corporate level, I have helped businesses create cultures around pursuing organizational greatness.

Over the years, I have seen many, many unhappy people with unrealized potential. Somewhere along the way, they became miserable and decided to stay that way. Misery's familiarity often feels easier and more comfortable than change. Comfort is the enemy of greatness. Life can be fraught with sadness and desperation, interspersed with intermittent glimpses of joy. When people don't understand how to integrate all areas of their lives, they live "boxed in." Their lives are like a series of storage warehouses piled to the top with old, discarded junk that serves no purpose. That storage bill has to be paid every month. It's a constant reminder of our stunted growth and the junk that lingers in our life. Our best and highest cannot be developed in the midst of confusion and emotional clutter. We find ourselves not being able to integrate who we are at work, at home, in the community, and so on. Our boxes pile up, and we never discover the bridge that leads to a well-integrated life. There is no sense of how to take those wonderful gifts and talents and have them spill over into every aspect of our lives. Your gifts and talents can permeate and mesh all that is special about you into everything you do on a daily basis. Your gifts and talents can lead you to your calling and your assignment on the earth.

In this book, do not expect twenty-five steps on how to discover greatness. Do not expect forty thousand hours of intense research to support my theories—you won't find them. Frankly, I just decided to start writing and keep going until I didn't have anything else meaningful to say. I suggest you stop reading when there is nothing else meaningful for you to learn. With that kind of loose, organic approach to book writing, what can you expect to gain? You can expect the following: transparent wisdom of one person's lifelong journey to discovering her greatness, her assignment on the earth, and how to apply both practically to everyday living. Hopefully, you'll see the value of embracing your own life with more vitality and intentionality. You'll be introduced to concepts that you may have heard before, but you are now ready to embrace. It is said that when the student is ready, the teacher appears. Or, perhaps some insights may be nuanced or presented in such a way that it has a higher meaning to you. I purposely made this book short and easy to read. It will help you reconsider how you walk out the rest of your life by challenging how you think about yourself and how you think about your potential, your capacity, and your calling. A paradigm shift may be in order to help you reassess how you view your role in the world. What does your "wuz here" self-portrait look like?

Essentially, my gift is that of a teacher and a wisdom coach. You are one piece of wisdom away from living your best life. What hinders you from igniting your greatness? My earthly assignment is to help others gain clarity, so they can embrace the life they were purposed to live. A purposed life creates a multiplier effect on the world. It is living in such a powerful way that your energy and impact extends beyond your mortality. Your life will speak something valuable to the next generation and the next. Your time on earth will matter to someone other than you. George Washington Carver said, "No individual has any right to come into the world and go out of it without leaving behind his distinct and legitimate reasons for having passed through it."

This is a spiritual journey for all of us. Reconciling the spiritual and the practical allows your calling to be both effective and productive. It took me many years to decipher my own purpose and greatness. I suspect my journey was long so that I could teach you how to avoid certain pitfalls and embrace the right opportunities to ultimately enjoy the fruits of a purposed life. This book will help you learn to appreciate the person that is uniquely you. There may be sections of the book that you will need to refer to over and over again. Hopefully, you'll be inspired to labor to define your uniqueness, so you can live a well-integrated, exciting, called life filled with joy, purpose, and peace.

1

———

WHEN LIFE KICKS YOU IN YOUR KEISTER, GET YOUR #$% MOVING!

I USED TO CURSE LIKE A SAILOR! IT WASN'T something that I learned from my parents. They didn't use foul language, and we certainly weren't allowed to have a potty mouth at home. However, somewhere along the way, cursing became a way for me to amplify my anger and my misery. I wanted to let the world know that I was PISSED OFF about everything! I subconsciously knew that dropping F-bombs wasn't who I was, but I used it as a very poor coping tool to redirect my anger. In reality, all it did was fuel my anger. My anger about my horrible boss, my unfulfilling career, my lack of financial resources, and anything else I decided to throw into the boiling emotional pot. I felt on the edge and stressed, so much so that I would call in sick on Mondays and some Fridays. I justified calling in sick by saying to myself that I was indeed sick—sick of my circumstances. I didn't know what to do about any of it, but the Universe will reveal knowledge to you. However, you have to be willing to listen—even through the pain. My change came wrapped in sadness and grief. I was already at an all-time emotional low. I was probably clinically depressed, but didn't know it; or, I could have actually been homicidal! Either way, I was not whole, not powerful. I was exhausted by life. On December 24, 1995, I got a wake-up call—literally.

One event can transform your life. When I think about December 24, 1995, I often wonder if I would be the person that I am today if that event had not happened. I'm not sure that I can honestly answer that question, but I do ponder it from time to time. I'm certain that this tragedy transformed me, but I wonder if I would have had the courage to change without this tragedy. When my mom called me that morning, everything went dark; my soul screamed in confusion. Shirley was my mother's only sister: my aunt. She died of a massive heart attack on Christmas Eve 1995. She was thirty-eight. There was a ten-year difference in our ages, so we were more like sisters than aunt and niece. I loved her to the depths of my soul, and I still do. She brought laughter and joy to my world. She taught me how to dance to the Ohio Players and helped me create my first afro. She laughed out loud and created a pure joyous experience for everyone around her. She was always emotionally present which made people feel special and loved. I didn't realize until she was gone that I never saw her angry. Which is significant because before she died, I was (at the ripe old age of twenty-eight) angry and miserable virtually every day. As I mentioned, I was working sixty hours a week for a horrible boss doing unsatisfying work that I hated. On the bright side, the company was rich with opportunity, but I would later decide that my destiny would lie elsewhere. I decided that my dream of corporate domination would not satisfy my independent, creative nature. This confluence of anger and toxic living was taking a toll on my emotional health and my new marriage. Yes, somewhere in the midst of my sadness, I managed to meet my soulmate, my life-partner, my best friend. His love helped stabilize me, but I was pretty sure he wasn't going to be able to live with my kind of crazy forever.

Shirley's funeral was standing room only. This small country church was completely full of people who came to celebrate my aunt's life. You would have thought she was a head of state, but instead she worked at a factory on an assembly line. I'm a first-generation college graduate, and when I would come home from the university, she would put money in my purse or pocket without me knowing it. She knew I wouldn't take the money because I understood how hard she worked to get it. As I look back, I now understand that it was important for her to invest in me—to give to a greater purpose. It was important to her that I succeeded. That success was not just for me, but for others in my family that would come after me.

I spoke at her funeral. While writing my notes, I had already determined that I would make people laugh out loud. Their laughter would honor her life more than any other words I could say, so I told funny stories of her life and my time with her. When I went to the podium, I was deeply struck by the vast swath of humanity in the sanctuary. They had come to celebrate the life of someone who planted seeds of joy in their lives daily; it was her gift, her assignment, her meaningful work. As I pulled out my handwritten notes and started to speak, I knew that if I died the next day, I would be lucky if twenty people showed up at my funeral. I had become so self-absorbed, confused, and miserable that I was losing the essence of who God created me to be. I left the podium determined that I would change all of that. I would fight to take back my life before I was sucked down some black hole. I would discover what it meant to live a called, purposed, vibrant, powerful, and joyous life. I started by quitting my job two months after her funeral.

THE NON-NEGOTIABLES: ESTABLISHING YOUR PERSONAL MANDATES

I had a lot to emotionally process. My grief was palpable, and so was the grief of my family. It was as if someone had blown out the flame on a wonderfully fragrant candle that was a source of light and joy. With all of this emotion, I had to at least determine what I wouldn't do anymore. I needed well-defined standards for living. I needed to decide how I would handle my life from that point forward. I knew the right boundaries would keep me focused and on the right path. I wouldn't create any more crazy unnecessary regrets. In the year Shirley died, my husband and I had purchased our first home. She called me before Thanksgiving and wanted me to host our family's traditional Thanksgiving dinner. She knew I hated cooking, so she volunteered herself and my mom to do all the cooking. I turned her down cold. I told her that I had been working really hard and that we were going to the mountains for Thanksgiving, and I would see her on Christmas. I've never forgotten the sadness in her voice as she tried to convince me to change my mind. That was the last time I talked to her. That conversation has been a powerful motivator for me to maintain my mandates.

Sometimes, it's easier to decide what you don't want in your life. Deciding what we want can be overwhelming. I started with the things I didn't want. To stop cursing was high on the list! I wanted my words to matter and to empower people, not tear them down. That seemingly small change had a huge impact. I had to become accountable to myself for choosing thoughtful and empowering words. Not cursing was hard. Many of my friends cursed. I had to retrain my mind and replace the foul words with different words. Every time I felt the urge to curse, I replaced the foul word with "chicken butt." I have no idea why I used that substitute word, but it worked. It would be a couple of years before I stopped even thinking the foul words; they slowly diminished and eventually disappeared from my spirit. For the most part, they are gone! Every now and again, one might pop up in my mind if I'm really in a bad space, but that rarely happens anymore. That small change redirected my thought patterns not just about what came out of my mouth, but about what was in my heart. Your mandates might start out seemingly small, but don't underestimate the power of those small changes to change your heart.

I have three life mandates, or non-negotiables. I'm proud to say that I haven't disrespected or tossed any of them in over twenty years. Now, admittedly, I've come close; especially when it comes to putting my work before my family. That one can be a tremendous challenge for me because I'm a workaholic by nature, and my work is my calling, so it's not just nine-five for me. I'm energized and propelled by my work; it's knitted to my mind and my soul. So needless to say, I'll probably always struggle with that one.

MY PERSONAL MANDATES ARE

First, I will live my life in the correct order, so I won't experience unnecessary guilt and regrets. That order is faith (spiritual pursuit of God), family, and then work. Secondly, I'll not make life decisions based on money.

Even if I have to work at a low paying job to survive, money and materialism will not be the decision drivers that blind me to what is possible for my life. Finally, I will vigorously pursue my purpose or die trying. Period.

Without a personal life mandate, your daily living is clouded. Our mandates are rooted in our core values. If you don't understand your core values, you make decisions from a fragile, ungrounded place. Your mandates act as protective guardrails that keep you progressing towards right choices, self-credibility, and powerful self-discovery. Our life is a culmination of our choices. Self-credibility is being able to look one's self in the mirror without guilt and shame brought on by repeated poor choices that oppose your core values. Powerful self-discovery allows you to live confidently and comfortably with who you are. It is accepting and loving yourself, flaws and all, but also nurturing and leveraging your gifts and talents.

On the surface, it seems like it would be easy to come up with personal mandates. Your non-negotiables will require your conviction and your commitment. Conviction and commitment challenge all of us. I think it was only easy for me because I had a glaring revelation of loss in my life. I didn't know what I wanted exactly, but I was darn sure of what I would no longer accept as normal in my life. It wasn't normal to work all the time and take my family for granted. It wasn't normal to be near clinical depression on Monday morning because you didn't want to go to work. I was determined to create a new normal for myself. I would become the woman that the Great Spirit of the Universe had created me to be; I would not settle for anything else. So the journey began . . . and it joyfully continues to this day.

I'm a different woman now. Most of my days are rich in joy, and my mind and heart celebrate life's gifts daily. I'm grateful. Of course, it would be disingenuous if I didn't admit that there have been times when my own mandates seemed more like towering fortresses that hindered me rather than guardrails that guided my progress. But to date, I have no regrets. These three principles have served as night watchmen in my life. They protect the things that are truly important in my life.

Identifying your night watchmen or mandates is a powerful and necessary start to taking your life back.

We'll spend the rest of the book explaining why being patient with yourself is a necessary part of this often painful process. When you set your personal mandates in order, expect life to challenge your resolve. These challenges should be seen as building your character muscles. For those of you who say you don't have patience, you really need to read on more than anyone else. You have to be teachable on this journey. Patience, in all of its forms, is a key ingredient to you receiving wisdom from the Universe.

LIFE'S LEARNING CUES: CAN'T YOU TAKE A HINT? THE STRUGGLE IS REAL!

All of us will experience hardships in some form. No one escapes the inevitable. Oddly enough, many of these challenges began with the letter "D": Divorce, Dishonesty, Depression, Disability, Disillusionment, and of course the real big one, Death. There are others that fall under the devastation umbrella such as being laid off or terminated from your job, unexpected illness, etc. you name it. If you live long enough, one or more of the "D's" will knock at your door or the door of someone you love.

There are as many ways to approach the unexpected as there are people who encounter life's struggles. But when you boil it all down, there is only one decision that you have to make: Will I fight for my life, or will I die and get stuck in this dark alley? There has to be a moment in time that you mark your territory. There is a placeholder in time where you soberly, consciously, and courageously decide to go to war. I say war because that is exactly what it has to be. It is an internal war for your peace, your joy, your sanity, and the ability to live your best life. You can't dilly dally around with self-hate, depression, perceived failure, resentment, wrongly-placed blame, or any of those loathsome emotional monsters.

Two people can experience the exact same circumstance but make very different decisions about how to approach the situation. For example, one person who loses a job may go into a deep depression and allow that loss to crush his self-esteem, build toxic emotions, and disconnect him from his family. Another individual who loses the same job may be temporarily depressed but makes a conscious decision to ponder why he lost his job and then start to develop a plan to move his life. There are countless people who have landed on their feet after losing their job. They either found better careers or decided to start their own small business. Many wouldn't go back to their old job if they doubled the pay because in their pain and pursuit of better, they discovered that if you pay attention, the universe will bring you what you believe you deserve.

During the height of the Great Recession, I attended a statewide event that was sort of like a town hall meeting on unemployment. I met an unemployed man there that I will probably never forget. He was well dressed, well-spoken, in his early forties, and was overall physically attractive. However, he oozed bitterness. He told me some of his story. He had been out of work for several months. He had put in hundreds of job applications, but only garnered a few interviews. As I listened, and tried to encourage him, we ended up in a verbal volley. I would say something positive, and he would say two things negative. After a while, I just listened and eventually ended the conversation. Looking back, I should have told him what he needed to hear the most. He needed to know that his energy and emotional state were so toxic that it would be very hard for him to find any job. He needed to understand the source of his bitterness and anger, and I suspect the job loss was just a part of it. Not the root cause. I hope he found his way back to a good place. I'm hopeful because I sensed he had an ember of determination which seemed to be one of his strengths. Unfortunately, I'm not sure he had ever paid close attention to his strengths or weaknesses. His emotional I.Q. was low. In other words, he wasn't a student of himself. He seemed to live an "event-oriented" life, meaning he went from this event to that event to this task to that task. His efforts were reactive, not strategic. He diluted his energy by being scattered not focused.

SELF-DISCOVERY:
BECOMING A STUDENT OF YOU

The problem is that many of us don't become students of ourselves; nor, do we leverage or incorporate the learning that pain, sorrow, and challenges provide. Sadly, many of us don't truly believe that we deserve peace, joy, adventure, and happiness. We don't see life as the universe providing abundance; we live in mental and emotional scarcity. We don't take the time to examine our own unique abundance and define how we can make a contribution. Our God given creativity is our birthright. However, it gets squelched somewhere along the way, and we regress into panic or passiveness. In our Western world, we tend to only pay attention to the next thing, the next task, the next dollar. But, we don't pay attention to our greatest and most valuable asset: us. We are too busy going nowhere fast. We exist like a gerbil on a wheel who doesn't have enough insight or intuition to stop, take stock, and manage our life. We never give ourselves the luxury of pausing. Sometimes, it's because we might not like what we see, and other times, we are simply oblivious to the need to do something different. Discovery and development require our attention. They go hand in hand with living a rich, robust, meaningful life. When we are born, we are curious about who we are and why we are. Howard Thurman, the great social justice leader, said, "Don't ask yourself what the world needs. Ask yourself what makes you come alive and then go do that. Because what the world needs is people who have come alive."

I had a conversation with a colleague who is an organizational psychologist about the danger of severe low self-esteem in leaders. He agreed with my viewpoint, and then he went on to tell me that either I have had a lot of therapy, or I've been a codependent for a family member who has had a lot of therapy. I laughed my head off. It was one of the greatest compliments that anyone has ever given me. I told him that neither was the case, but that for as long as I can remember, I've spent a lifetime seeking God's wisdom about how to live my life in the best, most meaningful way. I'm probably about twenty years older in my spiritual maturity than my numerical age. I've simply paid attention as

I've walked through life. I've paid attention to me, my weaknesses, and my strengths, and I have always had a keen interest in what makes all of us whole and useful on the earth. My curiosity and observant nature has given me a heightened level of discernment, intuitiveness, and a high emotional I.Q., all of which honestly sometimes strikes me as a little weird. Discernment, intuitiveness, and my emotional I.Q. all help me with judgment and decision making. These intangible gifts increase as you use them. They are cumulative in nature, and they reflect how much a person has paid attention to all of life's learning cues. These learning cues produce wisdom, strength, confidence, and courage that give birth to peace, joy, adventure, and happiness. So what do you pay attention to first? Well, that is a great question.

THE THREE ENEMIES OF GROWTH

The mysteries that hinder our growth have to be uncovered. We have the internal power to do it ourselves but, often, we need help. Sometimes that help comes in the form of a good, honest friend or family member, or we may need a therapist or a coach to help us. Regardless of how you come to identify and clarify those roadblocks, it is imperative that you give "it" a name. Your emotional health and happiness will demand clarity at some point in the process. There are three enemies of growth. Your particular challenge will fall into one of these categories: fear, self-confusion, or laziness. Fear is the leader of the pack. It keeps you in a dark, cramped place. Your world is limited. Biologically speaking, fear is there to protect us from physical harm. It alerts us to danger. However, our mind perverts this wonderful gift of protection and uses it as a fortress that we can grow old behind. Some of us rarely venture out of this stronghold because we are afraid that there is an army waiting to destroy us. This destructive mentality keeps us from accessing fields of opportunity that can guide our growth and lead us to a path of freedom. What do you fear? Failure? Success? What have you thought about doing in the last few weeks, months, or years that you didn't do because of fear? Did you think you were too old, too dumb, too poor, etc.? What negative narrative have you created about yourself that hinders you from living your best life?

If fear is the leader of the pack, self-confusion or (to put it another way) lack of self-awareness is fear's right-hand man. If you are not a student of yourself, you'll never understand your negative emotional triggers; nor, will you fully understand your value and uniqueness. Your negative emotional triggers cause you act out based on fear. You'll stay on an emotional merry-go-round that plays the same sad song of, "That's just the way I am; I'm not going to change for anyone." Pay attention to why you get angry, why your self-esteem plummets when someone challenges your ideas, why you gossip at work, why you won't apply for the promotion, or why you won't start that side hustle. What is it that you don't know about yourself, and how much does your not knowing cost you?

Conversely, knowing what energizes you and what interests you is powerful. You know what to pursue and what to say yes to. You understand your value and your uniqueness, and you are willing to share what you have to offer with the world. Instead of feeling

limited, there is a sense that there are constant possibilities. The world opens up for you, and you begin to
plant seeds of greatness that will grow beyond your
lifetime. You have an abundant mindset. In this space,
you understand both your private self and public self.
Your private self should be closely aligned with who
you are publicly. We know from literature that a Dr.-
Jekyll-and-Mr.-Hyde existence never ends well. People
notice divisive, confused internal energy, and they will
also notice your wholeness. Wholeness is magnetic. I
can't count the number of times people have told me
that I have a "calmness" about me that makes them
feel at ease. I always smile when someone compliments
me in that way because, as I mentioned in the intro-
duction, that was definitely not always the case. There
is a peace that radiates from the deepest part of me. I
love the person that I've become. Of course, I'm still
evolving, but there is a level of contentment that comes
from accepting yourself fully. I'm far from perfect. God
is not surprised by my imperfections, but I do imagine
that He is excited when He sees me use the tools that
He has given me to live a "whole-ly live." The more I

pursue wisdom about myself and life, the more I gain wisdom. The less I pursue wisdom, the weaker and dumber I become. I also stop growing at the point I stop seeking. To stop seeking leads to you losing your relevancy, and your ability to have impact. Seeking to know more and to be more is a powerful currency that allows you to cash in on what life has to offer.

The word laziness conjures up a vision in our mind's eye. Laziness is many things, but for our discussion, it is a lack of self-discipline. Frankly, all of us have a lazy streak in some area. Of course, you may not identify it as such. But, if you really dig deep, you would agree. Self-discipline speaks to how proactive and strategic you are in successfully managing specific areas of your life. It is also the power of the habits you create, or those you need to create. Financially speaking, we all know that it is better to have a spending plan than to not have one. You have known that all of your life; however, you still don't have one, and your finances reflect that. Or, you are the world's greatest procrastinator. You can come up with twelve reasons why you haven't completed a project at work or at home. It has become comical to those who live or work with you. Or perhaps, you're always late. Unfortunately, all of these have actually become a character trait for you and not in a good way. If you could change one thing that would "cure" your self-destructive, lazy streak, what would it be? In the book, The Power of Habit, author Charles Duhigg talks about the keystone habit. A keystone habit is the one thing that you can change that changes everything else.

I taught a Sunday school class on finances a few years ago, and I asked the class, "If you could change one thing about your finances, that would change everything, what would it be?" I gave them the example of my drinking coffee. I stated to the class that if I stopped drinking coffee, I would eat fewer sweets. Why you ask? Because my morning coffee would always have creamer and sweetener in it, which would set me up to desire sugar which is addictive. The power of the mind is amazing. About a month after that particular class, I got up on a Saturday morning to make coffee, like I had been doing for twenty-five years. I was about to take my first sip, and I had a gag reflex. After that, I didn't have coffee for two years! I do have coffee from time to time now, but coffee no longer has a hold on me. Amazingly enough, I also don't eat nearly as many sweets! The power of you changing just one important habit in your life can make all the difference. That one change can change everything else for you. What areas could you change that would make a tremendous difference in your ability to grow both personally and professionally? Start asking yourself daily, "What should I do differently now that I want to . . ." Also ask yourself, "In what areas of my life do I need more self-credibility? In other words, where do I need to be able to trust myself more?" Self-disciple deepens our self-trust. For example, I can honestly say that I hate forced exercise, but I've been doing for years. I actually have a little notebook on my treadmill where I log my distance, calories burned, etc. That notebook goes back for years. (It's about time for a new one.) That notebook reflects my commitment (self-discipline) to staying healthy and managing my weight. Now, don't get me wrong, I'm not setting the world on fire when I'm exercising! But, my commitment to the act itself means I can trust me to be consistent in this area of my life. The three enemies of growth are nasty little boogers that hold us hostage in our self-made fortress, but the funny thing is, you have the power to push the gate open and walk out as free as a bird. Why don't you?

2

———

THE CYCLES OF LIFE: PLAYING BY THE NUMBERS

ALL OF US SHOULD TAKE THE TIME TO look at our life in the rear-view mirror. Let me be clear. I am in no way a proponent of dwelling on the past. However, the past is probably your greatest educational tool and encyclopedia on starting the study of you. Many insights can be discovered by thinking back on your childhood. You'll even be able to pick up bits and pieces of where your true interests, gifts, and talents lie. You will be able to understand more about your values and why you make the decisions that you make—good and bad. This information can help awaken your power and your internal fortitude. Your intrinsic attributes will serve as foundational pillars for your unexplainable joy and your ability to look at life with expectation.

When I coach people, I'll ask them two numbers: How long have they been in a particular job or role and, secondly, their age. Funny thing, I've never had anyone refuse to answer. On the contrary, they answer readily and with curiosity. I have to admit, when I discovered these life patterns several years ago, I was doubtful and skeptical, but I kept seeing these patterns repeat over and over again. I saw it in the work that I did for organizations who were trying to change their culture. I saw it in business cycles of entrepreneurs. Frankly, more importantly, I've seen these patterns in my own life. Recognizing the significance of the numbers 2, 3, 5, 7, and 8 in my own life has been a strong, life changing epiphany. Before we get into the numbers, let me preface this by saying this: These are Biblical numbers that I learned from going to church and listening to my pastor's sermons over the course of about fourteen years. This section doesn't cover all the numbers on the number line. So, if you are wondering about the numbers 4, 11, etc., they are not mentioned in this book. The numbers I discuss are the numbers that have been reinforced and "tested" by observing my life, the lives of others, and business cycles of organizations. I was excited when Malcom Gladwell, in his book *Outliers,* presented his theory that ten thousand hours of deliberate practice can lead to success. Although, many have set out to debunk Gladwell's theory as oversimplification, no one can argue that huge investments of time and commitment to one's craft are key components to gaining and sustaining mastery.

These numbers are a great starting place for you to figure out your current placement on life's number line. There are many great definitions of wisdom, but the one that I like the most I also heard from a minister. He said that wisdom is your ability to discern change: change in you, change in others, and change in circumstances. That definition has stuck with me for many years. I really like to be proactive in determining what is going on around me and inside of me. If I can stay on top of those two, I'm usually positioned to win. These numbers will give you additional wisdom about your life. They will help you gauge your growth and track your pursuit of your purpose. I'm not sure that these numbers apply to everything in life, but I'm certain that they apply to individual and corporate growth, change, and development. These numbers will give you an idea of where you are in a particular life process. By the way, we are talking about number of years—not weeks or days. These numbers reflect a life journey filled with multiple marathons; it is definitely not a sprint.

NUMBER TWO - PRODUCTIVITY, HARD WORK, AND INSIGHT

The number two represents productivity. Any time you start something new: a new job, a new role, a new venture, it will take you two years of hard work to gain a fundamental understanding of what you are doing. For all of the multi-millionaire contract CEOs who are hired to turn companies around, they won't know any more than anyone else. They may be brilliant and highly talented, but it will still take two years of immersing themselves in the culture, the processes, and understanding the people to gain the level of insight to make the best decisions. I was mentoring a very smart young man who was off to a great start after college. When he and I spoke, he was on his second job, contemplating his third. After he gave me several reasons for his job changes, I shared an observation with him. I told him that he has not given himself enough time to mature or gain mastery in anything. His impatience in the short term would be a detriment to his personal and professional growth. He said he wasn't happy. I told him that not being "happy" is not a good reason to give up and quit multiple jobs in a short time period. Happiness is a temporary chemical reaction that occurs when you go shopping or see a picture of a cuddly, newborn panda. However, joy, peace, and authenticity come from a self-knowing and serving a cause greater than you. It takes effort to discover these things about you. Furthermore, maybe changing jobs would not be the cure for his unhappiness; perhaps the answer to his happiness was in a deeper place.

Let me share a short story with you. One of my core gifts is that of a teacher. Even though I started teaching (in some form) at age fourteen, it took years (and a bit of self-inflicted trauma) for me to discover that gift. At fourteen, I started teaching eight and ten-year-olds in Sunday School. I also tutored kids at the library. It never occurred to me that teaching was unique or special to me. I just enjoyed sharing knowledge and wisdom. During my college undergraduate years, I decided I wanted to teach at the college level someday. Not because I thought I was a gifted teacher, but it seemed like a really cool career option when I retired; I never really plan on retiring. I checked into how long it would take to do a double major in English. It was going to take too long and cost too much, so I said at some point I would get my master's degree. It was a personal goal, not a pursuit for money, but just something I wanted to do for myself. Years later, I landed an opportunity to teach at my local college; the first class was a disaster! I taught English Composition; fifty percent of my students dropped the class in the first week! I so wanted to walk away and drop the class myself, but

I couldn't do that. I couldn't break my commitment to the students that stayed. Teaching that class was an uphill slog that I shall never forget—but that slog changed everything! I later realized that my determination to teach that first class, in an easy-to-understand way, led me to my gift. It wasn't really about teaching English, but any complex subject. These were mostly adult students who were terrified of being in school again. They worked in the manufacturing industry, and they were taking my class so they could improve their career opportunities. There was no way I could let down the few that had the courage to remain in the class. That experience opened my eyes to a part of me that I didn't understand, nor did I have any clue existed. I have since seen a few of those students who were in that very first class many years ago.

I was amazed when they shared with me how much the class helped them. I was humbled by the fact that, even at my lowest skill level as a teacher, I was able to touch someone's life. Your gift, whatever it is, has the power to make a difference even in its rudimentary form.

Discovering your true talent takes time, hard work, and intentionality. Let me also say, just because you are naturally gifted in an area doesn't mean you are a master in that area. You have to dig in and nurture and grow that gift. You can't quit every time you are frustrated, confused, or "unhappy." Stay the course and commit the energy and hard work that it will take. You can't sit on the sidelines and watch the world go by. You have to be fully engaged in your life. Self-discovery is like digging for treasure that's buried seven feet under the ground. If you stop digging at six feet, you won't discover the treasure. Your commitment to the effort of self-discovery is as important as your actual talent itself because the effort strengthens and educates you.

NUMBER THREE - MATURITY AND CLARITY: THE ARTISAN'S CANVAS

If you can get through the first two years of any endeavor, then your third year will yield a great payoff. Three is the number of maturity and clarity. The power of clarity should never be underestimated. Clarity lifts the fog and shines a light on the next steps that can propel you forward. It is important to note that you don't get to three if you aren't diligent and hard working during the first two years of the cycle. Clarity comes at a price. Remember, two is the number of productivity. All of that hard work has a way of meshing the tangible and intangible together to birth an artisan. Year three is where the magic starts to happen. Visions start to form; people come alive, and they gain focus. They have more content and context to craft an authentic vision. They are mature in their thinking; therefore, they are able to innovate and produce ideas and concepts that can be tested. They've gained enough knowledge and wisdom to create magic in their lives and in the lives of those they are connected to. I'm always amused by how people who are new to their "next" leadership position think that they are going to change their company or department overnight. These leaders scramble to prove themselves in ninety days or less. The reality is that they would be better served to give themselves time to transition. They also need to fully understand the people, the process, and the goal. Speaking of the goal, you may need a whole new goal because the old one is no longer relevant or best. Young adults who move from job to job every year or two never gain traction or confidence. Year three's clarity is a result of your immersion in that which you are trying to manifest. During that time, you are productive, energized, challenged, and your character and commitment are forged. There is a crossing over that allows you to win. Ask any successful entrepreneur about the process. I've never met one who didn't have significant challenges in their early years. Moments where quitting would have been much easier than working through the obstacles. Making it to year three educates you in a way that no other class or college can.

NUMBER FIVE - GRACE AND MASTERY: THE NEW NORMAL

Grace is an unexplainable knowing that you have been propelled forward by a powerful force in the universe. You have arrived. You are in the right place at the right time. Mastery and true power are developed in year five. This surreal culmination is forged by your previous four years of hard work. Those years increased your learning and maturity. Your determination to overcome challenges and your faith in yourself and others allowed you to solve critical problems, to mature, and to paint a vision and walk it out. This new stage becomes your new normal, and it is important that you properly leverage every aspect of this stage.

Year five is the most rewarding time in the process because you can see the fruits of your labor. If you allow yourself to be open to the possibilities, true building occurs and visionary greatness takes hold of your soul. You are in a position to achieve more than you have in the previous time period, but be warned, not realizing this powerful stage can lead to depression and confusion. Five is not a graduation, but instead it represents your ability to pass a really long and difficult test. Because of this, many can get lost in confusion and depression, or boredom, because they don't know what else to do; they lose focus. You can breathe a sigh of relief, but if you are not careful, you can plateau and start to experience fear, doubt, and uncertainty.

However, if you stand on all the wisdom and strength that you have gained, you will run the last leg of the race and accomplish more than you thought possible. New concepts and ideas will emerge and catapult you into closing out this seven-year cycle. Because of your growth during this intense time, you are smarter and better equipped than you have ever been. Your confidence is strong because of your previous investment of time and self. Your mental and creative muscles are bulging; don't let them atrophy. In all honesty, it's time to maintain, leverage, and prepare for the next growth stage. Because "seven" will complete this cycle.

During the two "in-between" years of five and seven, take the time to smell the roses. Your confidence should be at an all-time high. However, don't be lulled into a false sense of security; you'll need to ramp up your productivity as you prepare to close this season in year seven. Seven is the number of perfection and completion. Your spirit will start to chomp at the bit; restlessness will settle in and frustrate you. Now is the time to pause and take a broad view of what you've endured and accomplished. You are more connected to who you are than you were previously; there is great comfort, peace, and boldness in this knowledge.

NUMBER SEVEN - COMPLETION AND PERFECTION

Lucky number seven has been used as a cliché for many, many years. Seven represents perfection and the completion of a cycle. It is imperative to pay attention to this cycle in your life. We're not talking about getting rid of your spouse or your friends after seven years and picking another group of people to be in relationship swith; however, we are talking about your mental and spiritual growth. There are times in life where you need to grow and intentionally evolve. Your personal development hinges on your ability to know when it is time to go and when it is time to grow. This can be a dangerous time because most of us are hesitant to change. We talk ourselves out of the next important work because it represents the unknown. We also confuse the internal turmoil that usually comes along with year seven. Those external sources include having a bad boss, fights with friends, the company we work for changes the rules, and so on. While all of these issues may be valid, it's you that is being forced by the Universe to look at your life—to soul-search and examine the next steps of your journey. It requires you to be open to the possibilities. If you aren't careful, you'll create a weird narrative that parades around in your mind and becomes a barrier to you moving to your next season.

A few years ago, I had a conversation with a client who was a Vice President of a medium sized organization. I noticed that he had not looked like himself for a while. He was the type of person who really brought the sunshine wherever he went. People in his organization loved him. During our conversation, I asked him how long he had been in his current position, and he said about six and a half years. He said he knew he could do more and was becoming increasingly frustrated by the status quo. He felt stagnant. I assured him that this was normal and seasonal, and it meant that God was telling him that it was time to go or grow. Humans need ongoing, meaningful challenges connected to their purpose in order to develop their full potential. Just a few months later, this wonderful man would get a COO (Chief Operating Officer) position that allowed him to move into a new growth opportunity—essentially a new season.

Seven requires a lot of faith because ordinarily you'll contemplate doing something you've never done before. After leaving corporate America, I started my independent business journey as a healthcare consultant. I worked to help doctors manage their accounts receivables and cash flow. One day, I was on my way to one of my clients' offices, and everything changed. It was a pretty large medical complex. Just as I was about to place my right foot on the concrete sidewalk, I heard an almost audible voice say, "It's over." Now, maybe I'm a little looney, but since I didn't know what was over, I asked, "What's over?" I didn't get a response, but I did find out in due time. This particular client had been a great client for over five years, but I went in a few days later, after hearing God's voice, and told them that I would be leaving the practice. They asked me to stay, and I said I would for another few months, but ultimately, I didn't have the heart to stay another few months. I knew that the voice I heard on the sidewalk was truth. Even though this client had been a client for five years, I was actually in year seven of this cycle. Two years prior to gaining this client, I sold practice management software. That experience taught me that doctors weren't always the best business people, so even though I hated selling the software, I became pretty good at it. However, I became even better at helping doctors improve their cash flow and reduce their receivables. Eventually, I stopped selling the software and focused only on helping doctors improve their cash flow and reduce their A/R. My entire stint as a healthcare consultant was a seven year cycle. It was time to go or grow. In this particular instance, it was time to go—to move on.

There were a lot of good things going on in my life at that time. My daughter was a toddler. I had started teaching at my local college, which as I mentioned earlier had been a personal goal, but I didn't expect it to happen so soon. I wouldn't realize until years later that becoming an adjunct professor would position me to do the type of consulting work that I do today.

Even with the good things going on in my life during that time, I was getting bored and frustrated with the healthcare consulting work I was doing. I felt there was more I needed to do, but since my income was stable and on the upswing, there was no logical reason for me to quit and change course. I have to pause and say that sometimes money (either having too much or too little) has an unhealthy influence on our pursuit of our purpose. Money can drive our decisions for a happy life far too much. I knew in my spirit that my next adventure would reveal itself once I transitioned from being a healthcare consultant. That was my truth to pursue, but I needed a great amount of faith. I knew I wouldn't be able to embrace the next season until I took this weird leap of faith that I didn't understand. And although my faith had grown in leaps and bounds, this felt different. Before, I had some clue of what I wanted; this time, I had no clue whatsoever.

A few weeks after making this difficult decision to change course, I was standing in front of my church after service, and one of the older ladies asked me how I was doing. I just burst into tears, and she hugged me.

I told her I was confused, and I knew God was up to something, but I didn't know what. At the time, I knew nothing about life's seasons or the numbers I've put in this book, but I would later go back and do the math and determine that my stint as a healthcare consultant had run its course. It was not my ultimate destination. My season as a healthcare consultant had been an awesome time in my life. I had learned to sell. I discovered my skill as a strategist and problem solver. I discovered that when it came to business, I actually did have a strong mathematical mind, which was contrary to my struggles with Algebra in high school and college. Probably most importantly, I had proven that I could replace my income outside of corporate America. There were many other lessons and skills that were honed during that time period for which I am very grateful. I learned that I was entrepreneurially minded, and that I had some leadership skills. I also learned that I was a "counselor," as one doctor client called me. I have to admit that it would be many years before I embraced that doctor's words and became a coach. More than anything, this season built my confidence to know that the things I had dreamed about as a child and as a young adult were possible. I was finally on the right path—but to where? Of that, I was not sure, but during this time, I learned to have faith in myself and faith in my God. The unknown still made me uneasy, but it didn't scare me as much.

The next cycle would help me discover my true gifts. Hearing God's voice on the sidewalk that day made a strong impression on my heart. It signaled that my life was about to change and evolve. Honestly, I've not heard His voice that strong regarding the change of a season since. Now, don't get me wrong, I've received distinct directions over the years that have guided my life in powerful ways, but this time was probably the loudest. Admittedly, those were dark, confusing days, but that was just the "noisiness" of life. At my core, despite the fear, I knew I had to make the move towards the next season. Even now, when I feel myself getting bored or frustrated for an extended period for no logical reason, I start doing the math on my number line. I redirect that negative energy and seek God's wisdom on my next steps. I tell myself that a new beginning is right around the corner. My stomach always starts to do flip flops of joy because there is a knowing on the inside of me. A knowing that the seemingly crazy leap of faith I took all those years ago doesn't seem so crazy at all today. I've made a few other leaps since then, but the first one was the most powerful. The first one was so strong and powerful that it made an indelible impression on me and set the tone for how I would walk my life journey from that point forward. Now, new beginnings are always welcomed and exciting.

NUMBER EIGHT - NEW BEGINNINGS

Eight represents new beginnings. Interestingly enough, new beginnings can be electrifying as well as terrifying, but I assure you boredom does not exist in this stage. It is yet another season of learning and growth, but it is different because you should be wiser than you were in the last stage, and this wisdom gives you more confidence and courage than you previously had. And although this new beginning can be a little intimidating, you've experienced this feeling before, so you are more confident that whatever is on the horizon, you'll thrive and grow exponentially from the process.

If you look at the span of your lifetime, let's say you live to be ninety-one, you will have lived thirteen seasons. If you are smart, by the time you kick the bucket at ninety-one, you will be in your most brilliant state of mind. You will truly be your most authentic self. Even if your body is frail, your mind, soul, and spirit should be comfortable, content, and at peace. You won't look back and wonder, "What if I had . . . volunteered at the Boys and Girls Club? What if I had applied for that promotion? What if I had entered that marathon? What if I had written that book?" There are very few what-ifs when you live boldly and intentionally. Intentionality screams that you pay attention not only to your day-to-day encounters, but you also pause to pay attention to where you are on life's continuum. Where is your dot on the timeline of life? What season are you in? Probably the most important thing I can say about the number eight is that you should have confidence in the fact that the last season has prepared you for the next season. The more you walk this pattern out, the more you understand how it works. All of this matters if you want to live a robust, fulfilled life and die happy. Dolly Parton is one of my heroes. Her life has had an incredible impact on making the world a better place. She leverages all of her talents and gifts in ways that bless humanity. In her book, *Dream More,* she alluded to the fact that she'll just drop dead one day doing what she loves. I laughed out loud when I read this because, for years, that's been my prayer. When I go, I'll just drop dead living the life I love.

3

AGES AND STAGES OF LIFE

I'VE BEEN COACHING PEOPLE FOR NEARLY my entire life. Of course, I didn't realize coaching was part of my gift set until I was in my late thirties, early forties. Since then, I have put energy and effort into nurturing that gift. As a result, I have been privileged to coach people from all walks of life, all ages, and at all levels of their careers. Some years ago, I started to notice significant emotional and behavioral patterns related to a person's age. For the purpose of this book, we'll only go through the sixties. Not because life ends at sixty, but admittedly, that is all I can authentically talk about since I'm currently in my fifties. I suspect in ten or fifteen years, I'll have lots to say about the seventies, eighties, and even the nineties! Mind you, for as long as I can remember, I have been thinking about how to live well and end well, but right now, my wisdom does not extend beyond the sixties. In this chapter, we'll discuss the twenties, thirties, forties, fifties, and sixties.

THE TWENTIES: EXPLORATION AND EXPERIENCE

Oh, if you could be twenty again—NOT! Don't get me wrong, I loved my twenties. Life was full of possibilities, energy, and ambition for me, but generally speaking, most of us are clueless about so many things in our twenties. We are especially clueless about ourselves. The twenties are about exploration and experience. It is the time in your life where you learn new things and increase your skills. It is also the time when you, in theory, have the least amount of obligations and responsibilities. Typically, you are unencumbered by children, marriage, or mortgages, so you can make decisions that only impact you. That freedom allows you do things that you might not ordinarily do. In college, I had several internships. One of those internships resulted in a job offer before I graduated. There was only one caveat: I didn't know what city I would live in; I knew the state, but not the city. Since I was only twenty-two at the time, no kids, no husband, I could move anywhere, so I accepted the job offer.

Your ability to rebound is much quicker and easier in your early twenties; therefore, it is a great time to challenge yourself to do crazy, impossible things that will grow you and expand your experiences. Now, I don't mean being irresponsible, but gaining exposure to different ways of thinking. In my early twenties, I had the chance to go to New York City, Los Angeles, Chicago, Mexico, and the Bahamas. You may think that those places were not a big deal, but let me tell you, they were very big deals to the small-town girl! I was wowed by the diversity and the fast pace of New York, and I loved the beauty of California. All of this exposure helped me grow and expand my horizons about what was possible. The early twenties are a powerful time of learning and exploration. Then when people hit the age of twenty-seven or twenty-eight, they start to get restless as they move into their thirties. I've had the privilege of counseling many, many late twenty and early thirty-year-olds. They are actually my all-time favorite people to mentor and coach because they are at a crossroads, and if they choose wisely, their lives can be robust and forever fulfilling. If they choose poorly, they may end up with regrets in their forties and fifties. We'll look at this phenomenon next in the thirties.

THE THIRTIES: PURPOSE AND PASSION

By the time I was thirty-two, I had established my business on a small level in that I had replaced my corporate income. I was one class away from finishing my master's degree, and I had my beautiful daughter. Twenty-eight to thirty-two was a whirlwind for me. I had gained a lot of good work experience in my early twenties. I had gained experience from three jobs. The first job was for five years, the second job was about a year, and the last job was about a year and a half. Moving into my thirties was a tumultuous time of confusion and uncertainty. I was unsure of my next steps, but I knew for certain that I wanted to control my own destiny. I wanted to be free to be creative and not feel boxed in and held captive by my own thoughts or other people's ideas. Essentially, I was evolving internally and seeking the next season.

Your twenties should prepare you for your thirties. The thirties are about finding your purpose and passion. There is a strong desire to know why you are on earth. In your twenties, you learn and grow, and perhaps you don't know what you want. But in the process of living out your twenties, you start to get some understanding of what you DON'T want. Interestingly enough, knowing what you don't want can be a powerful move towards reaching your deepest desires. It is the start of you discovering your talents, gifts, passion, and purpose. I had started to feel trapped and unhappy. At the time, I didn't realize that I'm one of those people who craves frequent opportunities to problem solve and be creative. I need space to dream, imagine, and reach for the stars. The problem with the thirties is that if no one explains to you that it is normal to be confused and frustrated, you may make mistakes or missteps, such as blaming your boss or your close acquaintances and family. You fail to recognize that your internal voice is screaming and prodding you to grow, and no one can change your circumstances except you and the Universe. You also have to understand that being patient is part of the process of becoming more centered so that you can focus and move forward. It's one of the best times in life to take a calculated risk that feeds your spirit, fills you with energy, and fuels your imagination. The thirties can be filled with with lots of trial and error, but with each trial and each error, you learn something that you need to know about yourself. You start to accept that you are special and unique. You become a little less self-focused and begin to venture out and see what else the world has for you. Your curiosity springs forth, and you start to connect the dots of your past experiences and your future options.

THE FORTIES:
BALANCE AND BOUNDARIES

Ahhh, the forties. The forties are wonderful years of raising kids, career building, and cementing who you are as a person. The number forty represents transition. You are transitioning from a moth into a beautiful butterfly. For most of us, when we turn forty, we'll have nearly twenty years of some type of work experience behind us. Usually, we have had at least one significant love relationship in our life, and regardless of whether it turned into a life partnership or not, the experience educated us about love. Forty is definitely a time of celebration, and it is also a time where we truly search for balance and the proper boundaries. Forty represents the halfway point in our lives, and we realize that our energy and physical stamina will not be what it was in our twenties. We start to see little differences here and there. A gray hair here, a slight laugh line that wasn't there five years ago and so on. Mainly, we start to realize that the things we cared about in the previous ten or fifteen years don't hold the same value. We start to contemplate what is really important to us at this stage in life. For some people, they start to realize how important family is as they see their parents start to age and see their children transition into adulthood. Or, perhaps for others, they have worked crazy long hours and have missed many of their children's events, and they start to focus on spending more time with their family. Whatever the case, this is the time to say yes to the right things and no to the things that no longer bring value. It's a time to refocus your life, so you can have laser vision when it comes to how you'll spend the next half of your life.

The forties demand self-examination. It's the time to ask yourself important questions like, "How can I be more effective in every area of my life? How can I move from quantity to quality life moves?" In theory, you should be smarter and wiser than you have ever been, so now is the time to take charge and forge a direction for the next forty years that makes sense for who you are and who you are becoming. Establishing balance and boundaries is key.

The word "balance" is a mystery to most of us; it gets batted around a good bit as a life solution. In my world, balance equates to harmony. Harmony allows us to create a world where balance can exist. A life where work, play, and relationships are in harmony. So, perhaps a more harmonious style of living should be the goal. In order to create harmony, you have to take inventory of your priorities and your burdens. Are you doing things to please other people? Are there activities that you are not suited for that you continue to volunteer for simply because you've been volunteering for the last five years? Do your weeks just rapidly fly by, leaving you at a loss to articulate what you've accomplished, felt, or created?

In my late forties, I reduced the time I spent volunteering in my community. I decided that one of the most precious items that I must have stewardship over is my time because it is rapidly in short supply. One of the boards I served on never felt quite right. It was cliquish and geared primarily towards fundraising, and although we did some great work, I didn't enjoy being on the board nor did I enjoy the people. They were wonderful people, but I wasn't a good fit. The other board was one that I had joined because a mentor, whom I love and hold in great esteem, had asked me to join. I simply couldn't say no to her as she had been a significant influence in my life. This particular board wasn't in my wheelhouse so to speak, but I must say it was, without a doubt, a great board with a great mission. My mentor retired, and my reason for being on the board left with her. There are a couple of other obligations that I had to cull from my life, and there are two reasons I removed this extra "fluff" out of my life: my daughter and my focus. My daughter was entering her teenage years, and she needed me more than ever. Secondly, I wanted the last half of my life to have an even greater impact. Therefore, I needed to focus more on my strengths and my earthly assignment. As a part of taking inventory of my priorities and burdens, I could channel my energy better. As a result, I learned to quickly say no to those things that don't line up with my calling or that interfere with family time. Doing this close self-evaluation has allowed me to say yes to those life-giving, world-changing opportunities that await me. My boundaries keep me focused and help me conserve my time and energy. For example, I very rarely will say yes to any evening events or obligations through the week because of my daughter's school schedule and because talking to her about her day is important to both of us. My love for my husband and my daughter are my most precious gifts from God. I simply refuse to wake up at ninety and regret having not made them a priority in my life. Additionally, I've always felt the spiritual tug to make sure my life on earth counts for something greater than me, so the pursuit of that cause is a part of my DNA. Those two drivers (my family and my desire to live a life of impact) were all established solidly in my forties. I feel more authentic, more empowered, and more comfortable in my own skin than ever before. Not feeling encumbered to do things that don't connect with who you are, or where you are going, is truly a refreshing way to approach life.

THE FIFTIES: EMPOWERMENT AND ENLIGHTENMENT

Fifty represents jubilee; it's a celebration of your life. The fifties bring enlightenment. Enlightenment is a type of spiritual revelation that opens your eyes in new ways about you and the world. Truths that you have pondered for years finally make sense. You can breathe deeply and be invigorated by your senses and your life choices. You can celebrate life in a way you didn't have the wisdom to do in earlier times of your life. You are empowered to discover more about yourself and how to live your best life. You are empowered because you are less risk averse and less self-conscious. I've heard it said that you are not even close to being smart until you reach the age of fifty. Because you've worked out some of life's kinks, and have more wisdom, your fifties can be some of your most productive years. Of course, the fifties are productive only if you've done a good job of walking through your previous life cycles and stages. If you haven't, that's okay. You just have to play catch up the first few years—the first three years to be exact. The great thing about your fifties is that your focus and clarity are phenomenal. You've gained an understanding of who you are as a person, and you should know and fully understand your skills and talents. Therefore, you are able to apply and leverage all of your attributes like never before. For those of us who are intentional during this season, your personal growth can be rapid and exponential. You are now "stable" enough to handle life and wise enough to make good judgments about yourself, others, work, and the list goes on.

Good judgment is a precious asset that is earned over time. Your wisdom and good judgment come from everything you have paid attention to in your lifetime. The good times, the failures, the pain, the mediocrities of both yourself and others all give us knowledge to build upon. That knowledge, coupled with our God-given intuition, advises us on when to move and when not to move, when to be quiet and when to be loud. So much of life's rich lessons are taught in the trenches. I'll never forget the good business lessons I learned from a couple of bad bosses. Indirectly, they gave me the courage to start my own business because I knew their behavior was not how I wanted to live my life. When my aunt died, I learned to appreciate living on a deeper level. My grief was profound, and yet it was the emotional catalyst that propelled me to fully explore my life.

At fifty, all of your experiences, education, knowledge, and emotions culminate to create a perfect strain of DNA that is uniquely you and that should be celebrated and maximized like no other time in your life. You'll make an indelible mark on the world that only you can make. The world can be different and better because you are in it. During your fifties, you can contribute in ways that you never could before. Carpe diem! Seize your days; be carefree, but not careless. Impress yourself, not others. When you look in the mirror, smile at the reflection that greets you. That rich reflection represents the essence of who you are—all decked out in your strengths and weaknesses. Recognize the imperfections; yet realize that even your imperfections are purposeful. Acknowledging our imperfections keeps us humble, self-aware, and believable.

In your fifties, you can sense the strong role that peace plays in our life. Peace is a place of centeredness and power; it has no counterpart, but it does give birth to joy. Embrace your fifties with expectation. Know that you are better than you've ever been. You can go roaring into your sixties, where you will start to craft your legacy.

THE SIXTIES:
ACCEPTANCE AND LEGACY

I must admit that I don't know as much as I would like to about the sixties. But I've done some research, and what I've discovered from those who live in this season is that it can be a very vibrant time of life. You hold precious grandchildren, and you start to slow down and reflect more. I had a very wise woman tell me (she was sixty-five at the time) that the sixties were about acceptance. Her words rang true to me. It's past time to release any negative emotions such as guilt, resentment, anger, and so on. This is a time where you look at your mistakes as a part of your journey. If you had a failed marriage, or your children chose a path that you were opposed to, you let go of all of that and forge on to this last third of your life. You should have more time to leverage and apply your gifts. Time to continue to produce and help others grow. You can mentor those who are coming after you. This is the time that you start to think seriously about your legacy. Legacy living simply means that you continue to plant seeds that will outlive your lifetime. As a retired teacher, you could volunteer at the local library and tutor children whose parents cannot afford a tutor. As an entrepreneur, you could take green entrepreneurs under your wing and help them become successful. The sixties are really the time to embrace your legacy and focus on investing your time and energy in a way that will grow beyond your lifetime. This focus will keep you energized and engaged in life in a way that will help you continue to live with gusto as you age.

Several years ago, my husband and I were sitting in an open air pavilion in Arizona waiting on our Grand Canyon tour bus. While sitting outside, I overheard the conversation of two elderly couples. I couldn't guess their ages, but they were nearing or in their eighties. One man said, "Yeah, the sixties are pretty good. I still played softball in my sixties." The other man responded, "You're right, the seventies are okay too, if you keep your health." Then he continued on and said, "But those eighties can get pretty rough; you can tell things are winding down," and both men laughed. It wasn't an uncomfortable laugh; it was a knowing laugh that life on this earth is temporary. It will wind down for all of us at some point. The tone of the conversation between the two men was funny and telling. It was nice to eavesdrop and gain wisdom from these two. As we all headed to our respective buses, I saw one of the men gingerly help his wife onto the bus. They both moved slowly, but she was the slower of the two. Both smiled at each other in a loving, knowing way. I didn't say anything to my husband, but I did feel a lump in my throat. I was in awe of the couple's love and tenacity for life. It was as magnificent as seeing the Grand Canyon itself.

When I was a child, I loved to spend time with my grandparents and great aunts. I had a sense that they knew more than me, and I wanted to know what they knew. As I move closer to the age they were when I was a child, I now understand that their knowledge was a result of living, not just aging. Wisdom does not come with age, but it comes by living an intentional life—a purposed life.

4

———

THE DEMYSTIFICATION OF DISCOVERING YOUR PURPOSE

PURPOSE IS NOT MAGICAL, BUT IT IS MYS-terious. All mysteries hold truths that have to be revealed. If we could demystify purpose and see it as a practical part of living, we would be more joy-centered and energized. Knowing our purpose helps us direct our day-to-day energy in a more productive, positive way. That understanding helps silence the noise in our life and helps us prioritize what is truly important.

Let's start by demystifying the word purpose. We've come to believe that purpose is a single, life focus that makes impacting the world part of the equation. While I believe that purpose is always connected to our humanity, it certainly doesn't always have to be global and feel daunting and unreachable. Purpose is tied to a couple of things. First, it's tied to our natural wiring, which are our gifts and talents. These intrinsic attributes seem to have no rhyme or reason, but they separate us from our neighbors and make us uniquely different. Secondly, our formative experiences shape our values and worldview. Those experiences create our truths and passion for life. We act out and behave from both of these wells.

When you look at a young child, you'll start to see patterns of behavior that indicate an aptitude for art, music, sports, or engineering. They seem drawn to a particular activity, and you'll see them smile or be excited when they are involved in this activity. That is a sign of their gifts emerging and a part of their natural wiring becoming functional and relevant to who they are. Taking notice of this metamorphosis is a great way of encouraging this growth in children. As we grow into adulthood, there are many stages of development, and sometimes, our natural wiring gets marginalized by others or by ourselves.

Unfortunately, as we age, who we are and what we are good at can become murky instead of clearer. It was simple when we were children because our unique creativity was fueled by instinct. As we age, depending on our influences, we become more cautious and more risk averse. Being realistic about risk is healthy and natural; however, being too risk averse can become self-defeating. When self-doubt and unsupportive voices creep in, fear takes the driver's seat. Fear, if allowed to take root, generates internal turmoil and confusion that clouds our thinking, challenges our confidence, and limits our courage. Ultimately, our fire for living is dampened.

When I coach, I'll often ask people to tell me about their current hobbies and the activities they enjoyed during childhood. What I find most disturbing is that many people have disconnected themselves from those joyful activities and have no adult interests that feed their gifts and talents. They have allowed themselves to be molded by external influences instead of their internal power. Life is lived on autopilot, and people inadvertently squeeze themselves into a rigid mold that suffocates their joy and energy. This act of disconnection stunts our growth and understanding of our magical, natural gifts.

Our gifts are not limited by physical location. Gifts and talents have universal value. If you are naturally organized, you'll add value whether you are in a civic organization in Brazil or in a Fortune 500 company in New York. If you have a creative eye, you will bring a certain uniqueness to a project that no one else can. We'll talk more about gifts later, but connecting to our gifts and talents leads us on a self-discovery journey that lands at the feet of our purpose.

In addition to our gifts and talents, our formative years and life experiences give birth to our purpose as well. During our lifetime, we receive information and engage in experiences give us our values. The first twenty years of our life are particularly important in forming our worldview and values. Our truths about fairness, right and wrong, justice, and humanity all stare us in the face and fuel our passions. Passion has been defined in many ways, but one that has stuck with me is that passion is a combination of two emotions: love and hate. We act out and behave from both of

these life wells. In the context of purpose, this definition makes sense. In our early years, we received nurturing, attention, and information that fed our soul and
spirit. Or, we didn't receive things that we needed to
feed our soul and spirit. Some of us were greatly supported and loved by those who raised us, and some of
us had love and support withheld from us. Our environment and culture play a great role in what we believe
is important.

When our values collide with our natural wiring, we
get closer to understanding our purpose. For example,
if you grew up in an impoverished household where
resources were scarce, you may become a very frugal
adult who is a good money manager. Or, you could
take the opposite approach, and continue the cycle of
poverty by spending every dime you get your hands
on and not managing your money. Either way, you've
made a subconscious decision about your relationship
with money. Your beliefs and values about money were
shaped in your childhood, and they influence how you
handle money as an adult. In this same scenario, let's
say the person who becomes the good money manager
decides that poverty is no longer acceptable for him

or his family. He decides to work towards building wealth. He eventually becomes financially successful, and that success changes his life. Somewhere along his life journey, he feels compelled to help others know that it is possible to defeat poverty. He decides to teach a personal finance class, and later he starts a non-profit organization to help others escape poverty. Year after year, his passionate efforts touch the lives of others. He helps generations of people come out of poverty. This is an example of how a person's past experiences can shape and define their passion. Eventually, he realizes that eradicating poverty is one of his primary purposes on earth, so he spends the rest of his life dedicating time, resources, and energy towards eliminating poverty.

Very few people know that President Jimmy Carter once lived in public housing. After his father died and the business his father left him failed, President Carter and his family lived in public housing. People talk about President Carter not being very effective during his term as President of the United States; however, no one can dismiss the fact that he has been a great humanitarian. His work with Habitat for Humanity has been awe inspiring. I often wonder if his passion around Habitat was shaped by his experience of living in public housing. Having a clear purpose gives you a single-mindedness that brings clarity to your life. You can better understand your existence, and you become keenly aware that your time is limited. Time is the great equalizer. No matter how rich you are, how poor you are, how handsome you are, everyone gets twenty-four hours in a day—no more, no less. You get to decide how you will spend that precious time. How will you spend the rest of your time? Procrastinating and pontificating, or will you spend it living on purpose?

We often look for big, monumental, grandiose leaps into purpose. Discovering your purpose is a gradual inching along. It is tedious because we have to be mindful, and we have to take the time to reflect. Purpose is attached to how we are wired, what we value, and how we disperse our energy to impact the people and issues we care about. Whether that is helping one person or a thousand people, our purpose has a multiplier effect that gives our lives meaning by connecting us to humanity and elevating our spirit and soul for our unique journey.

5

———

SELF-TRANSFORMATION

I T USED TO BOTHER ME TO HEAR PEOPLE talk about their purpose and passion. Purpose and passion felt so elusive to me; so out of reach. Both sounded like something for people who have a sixth sense, and the rest of us just have to pick up the pieces as best we can. Or worse, you never even get close to finding anything that slightly resembles purpose or passion. I love numbers and systems. I truly believe that God has a system for living. All of the answers we need to live our best life are available, but we have to actively seek the answers. For many of us, we simply don't pursue understanding our passion and purpose, or we give up too soon. I'm convinced that the earlier you start seeking, the sooner you will know. The very act of seeking positions your soul, mind, and spirit to be open to new revelations about you. Seeking puts you in partnership with the Universe and announces your great faith in the process of discovering your best self.

I remember my first real job being trained by this wonderful Christian woman. She had teenage children at the time, so she was several years older than me. I would have been about twenty-two. We were driving somewhere, and I remember telling her that I wasn't exactly sure what I would be doing in the future, but I didn't think it would be what I was doing at that time. In other words, I didn't think I would be with that particular company doing that particular job. She gave me a smile of agreement. About twenty-five years later, I saw this same lady at a funeral of someone we both knew. I asked her if she remembered our conversation in the car that day, and she said she absolutely did. I told her that I had found my purpose, and I was living it. She told me that there was no doubt in her mind that I would. I certainly don't think that I was or am special in any way, but I had a conviction about fully knowing all about me and why I was created for this time on earth. I wanted to know how I could contribute. We are all born wanting to know why. But, when time passes and we don't get a lightning bolt answer, then we ask less and less. Eventually, we don't ask at all, and sadly we give up all together. It is in this space that many of us decide to exist; we give up living. Every day is like the day before.

In 2011, I was preparing to speak to a group of women on courageous leadership, and I needed something profound and visual that I could deliver in about twenty-five minutes. So, I did what I often do when I'm clueless, I prayed. I prayed for an easy-to-understand concept that explained what it meant to be a courageous leader. Well my prayer was answered, and I created the "Transformation Model." In hindsight, the talk probably should have been called "Courageous Living." It was well received; so much so that I expanded it and incorporated it into my coaching process and practically all of my teachings, trainings, and mentoring. I have used this model to transform my own life, bit by bit, year after year, decade after decade, but I had no idea at the time that I was actually creating a formula for myself. Of course, the formula isn't just for me, but it is for every person who wants to discover their purpose, passion, assignment, and become their powerful, authentic self.

Onions are great in all kinds of recipes. They give flavor to any dish. However, if you've ever cut a strong onion, it can cause you to cry as you cut through its many layers. Cutting a strong onion is a visual for what true transformation looks like. Transforming yourself can cause you to cry. Like the onion, our lives are multi-layered; therefore, transformation can be time consuming and extremely difficult. Also like the onion, if we can get through the tears, we can use the experience to create our own flavorful recipe for living. Transformation allows us to build our self-esteem, realize our talents, mitigate our weaknesses, have the courage to take risks, and become more resilient. Transformation is powerful; it guides us to becoming our best, authentic self.

Self-Transformation Model

Copyright NGCEE 2011

SELF-DISCOVERY — THE SEARCH FOR YOUR AUTHENTIC SELF

In the center of an onion is its core. Each layer that grows is connected to the core. The growth process starts with the core. Our core should be ongoing self-discovery. Self-discovery is a lifestyle. It is the commitment that we will continue to grow and learn more about ourselves throughout our lifetime. We become students of ourselves. Unfortunately, we often mold ourselves around what others want us to be. In other words, we allow ourselves to be defined by external sources, rather than our own internal force. Think about the choices you've made over your lifetime. How many of those choices were based on what others thought you should do or be. A dear friend of mine majored in computer science many years ago because her dad thought it would be a guarantee on getting a good job. The reality is that my friend is really an amazing poet. She should have majored in the Humanities. Luckily, she has found her way back to her love of the written word. John Quincy Adams (the sixth president of the United States) said, "There are two educations. One should teach us how to make a living and the other how to live." Focusing on "how to live" is key to our inner joy.

AWARENESS—NURTURE AND MITIGATE

In my coaching practice, I always have the coachee take an assessment that helps identify his or her behaviors and values. With this information, I can help guide them through the process of identifying their strengths and their weaknesses. Everyone has strengths which can also be called gifts and talents; however, many of us neglect nurturing those gifts. If we nurture our gifts and talents, they grow and become powerful. When we ignore them, they atrophy—or worse yet—we don't even recognize them.

When I'm speaking to a group, and I ask them to list their gifts and talents, I usually get things like, "I'm a people person" or some other vague notion. More often than not, I get some weird job description, or a dumbfounded look. Because I'm highly discerning of individual energy and giftedness, I know that they really haven't consciously thought about their gifts and talents. When you don't consciously connect to your talents, you don't understand your value in the marketplace or elsewhere. This disconnect impacts your self-esteem over the course of your life. Remember how I talked about when we are children, we are instinctively drawn to activities that we are gifted to do. I talked to an engineer who said when he was a child, he would take all of his toys apart, and he continued this trend into high school, and parlayed it into a career as an engineer. He still likes to take things apart, but now it's on a much larger scale. Our potential is locked up in our gifts and talents. Those talents are naturally recurring behaviors that we are drawn to without any real explanation attached. They are magnetic in our spirits. In other words, we can do "x," but we have no real idea how or why we do "x." Interestingly enough, other people may recognize our gifts and talents before we do. People will come to you and ask you to help them, or they may want your expertise in a certain area. I actually became a coach because clients kept asking me to talk to employees and help them work through certain issues. It was quite a while before I realized that I had been sharing wisdom with people practically my entire life. I never saw it as anything special, because it was my normal. You probably don't see your gifts as anything special. You figure everybody can do "x."

My husband once took our daughter to a outdoor sporting event. They had a bow and arrow contest. Our daughter was eleven years old at the time. She picked up the bow and arrow and hit a bullseye on the first try. My husband was amazed and so was I! She later joined the archery team in middle school, and she became a pretty proficient archer. She never saw her ability as a talent, and she didn't like being on the team, but she did gain insight into one of her gifts. She has great hand-eye coordination and spatial giftedness, which supports what she is passionate about—she's a creative. I remember how quickly she would make jewelry when she was just five or six years old. Even though she didn't pursue archery as a sport, she gained great learning from the experience. You should challenge yourself to engage in opportunities outside your comfort zone. Exploration and experience will give you more insight into you. My daughter still has the bow and arrow she used while on the team. It was a pretty expensive set. We told her that she could donate it or sell it. So far, she has decided to keep it; it holds a special place in her heart. It gave her insight into her gifts.

The other side of the coin is discovering our weaknesses. Our weaknesses fall into a couple of categories. Often a weakness is a strength over-extended. For example, you can be a highly detailed person which is truly a gift. But, if your level of detail hinders you from making timely decisions because you need perfection, then your gift loses its value and becomes a barrier. These habits need to be examined and changed. In the case I mentioned, a person may have to be sure to put deadlines in place to speed up their pace, or they may need an accountability partner. The second category is a little trickier to resolve. This second category is where we have unhealthy, self-sabotaging emotional patterns that become liabilities to us in all of our relationships. Sometimes these can be character flaws. Several years ago, I was somewhat exasperated by a very brilliant executive leader. We were working on changing the culture to position the organization for future growth. I finally told him that he was a bully. He stopped cold, and said, "I hate bullies." I told him that may be the case, but that he exemplified bully traits on a daily basis. Sometimes, we unknowingly exemplify traits we hate because they have become our personal mode of operation, and no one ever has the guts to tell us our weakness, or what hinders our effectiveness.

Our weakness can become a liability if not dealt with properly. Life is funny. We develop unhealthy coping skills in our childhood that we spend all of our adult life trying to understand and unpack. Some of us may need therapy to reveal the deep-seated wounds of our past. Those wounds have to heal in order for us to truly be whole. They cause us to act out in toxic ways that strain our relationships and cause us to be disappointed in ourselves. Toxic emotions such as unresolved resentment, anger, pessimism, distrust, and passive aggressive behavior all hurt you and hurt others. Or, sometimes we turn our toxic emotions inward and self-destruct or disconnect from the world. This type of behavior is the most insidious of all because we are all wired for relationships and community. Perhaps, you are so shy and introverted that you never gain the courage to share your thoughts or ideas, so they just stew inside and die with you. You've never taken the time to discover your superpower and how to release it so that it can flourish and make an impact. People that I coach know that I'll tell them the hard truth. I have found that most people do want to hear it . . . if they are ready.

Sometimes readiness comes in the form of losing your job, your marriage, or some other devastating relationship loss such as death of a loved one. One of my favorite shows, *Hoarders*, explores how people are able to live in complete and utter squalor. I'm fascinated by the show and will binge watch it on occasion. Sometimes people get stuck because they have experienced trauma that they typically couldn't control, and the event stops them from living. The "stuff" hoarders cling to represents their cluttered emotions and their attempt to control their small, limited world. I think I love the show because I know that any of us can get stuck. We may not have a visible representation such as hoarding, but when we stop living and seeking to be our best selves, we are stuck. When we are no longer curious about life and shut out the world, we are as stuck as much as the person who hoards.

Understanding your weaknesses and emotional triggers are just as powerful as embracing your gifts. Your weaknesses, which I call your less evolved self, can derail your life. On some level, your gifts will naturally emerge. But your weaknesses hide in the crooks and crannies of your mind and soul. They are shape shifters who deflect, place blame, and shield themselves from truth. If not managed, they will eventually yield destruction. There is no shame in acknowledging our limitations and weaknesses. The converse is true. There is great wisdom and power in knowing and understanding both your strengths and weaknesses. This knowledge frees you to become more of who you are. You are able to set up healthy boundaries, so you can allow light to shine in your life and protect the best parts of you against the enemy.

CONFIDENCE—TRIAL AND ERROR

Many think that confidence starts in childhood and then ends somewhere in your twenties or thirties. Nothing could be further from the truth. Growing your confidence is a lifelong endeavor. You should be more confident at forty-five than you ever were at twenty-five. Strong confidence is a sign of someone who has toiled, learned, and persevered. Confidence is truly a process of trial and error. It is small successes built upon small successes. For those of us who have children, it is wonderful parenting to give them ongoing encouragement and kind words; however, you do them a disservice when you don't allow them to try and fail and pick themselves up again. I hesitate to use the word failure because it is really a part of the learning process. Struggle is part of the expansion process; every part of you is educated through struggle. You gain greater knowledge, emotional fortitude, and even skills. We all run from taking risks, when those risks are our greatest teachers. Whether or not we win is anyone's guess. I had a conversation with my daughter about regrets. I told her that I have very few (if any) regrets at this point in my life. There are certainly a few people and situations that I wish I had avoided, but when I look at the totality of my life—I took risks in areas that mattered most to me.

As I mentioned to you early on, after I received my master's in English, I thought I'd try my hand at teaching part-time at the local college. My first class was a disaster! Half of the students dropped the class, and frankly, I wanted to drop too! But because I have a strong work ethic, and the fact that my dad taught me to never break my word, I did not quit. I survived the class. Well, amazingly enough, the college called me back to teach a second class. I was determined that I would get better, and I did. In the beginning, most of the students were working adults who had been out of school for years. They were intimidated by the work, and I had to figure out a way to make it simple for them. Essentially, I had to teach myself how to teach which was an arduous process. But through that process, I created an online writing program which I was later able to make several thousand dollars off of! If I had given up because I was discouraged and felt inadequate (which I did feel both of those), I would have missed out on a tremendous amount of learning about myself. Oddly enough, it was during those times that I discovered one of my greatest gifts is being a teacher. Lord knows if you can successfully teach English to people who have been out of school for twenty years, you can teach ANYTHING! I also became a much better writer; anything you teach, you learn on a deeper level. My confidence as a teacher grew exponentially during that time, but it was A LOT of trial and error.

Nearly every year of my life, I take on "learning projects" that challenge me to grow more. By default, these learning projects help me continuously increase my confidence. I have to admit, I'm probably one of the most confident people you'll ever meet. First, I have confidence in who God has created me to be. And secondly, I see it as my responsibility to continue to nurture my gifts and grow my skills. That may sound a little arrogant, but it's not. Don't confuse arrogance with confidence; arrogance is counterfeit confidence. Those who are arrogant are afraid someone is going to find out the truth about them, so they do hurtful things when they feel threatened or challenged. These people more often than not have very low self-esteem which is the root cause of their unhealthy behaviors. Unfortunately, many of us have negative recordings playing over and over in our heads. These negative thoughts were placed there by a parent, a spouse, a bully, a teacher, and so on. But even so, only you can shoulder the responsibility for your life. You have to decide what tapes play in your head and how you react to life. True confidence is the building and exploratory process of gaining traction so you can create successful life outcomes. Confidence is like climbing a mountain; you inch along by putting your hands and feet in just the right place, and eventually, you reach the top.

COURAGE — THE POWER OF WHAT YOU VALUE

Confidence and courage are not the same. When I was preparing the courageous leadership talking points for my speech in 2011, I was stumped by what true courage actually means. We see war heroes and amazing first responders on the news. We study people like Martin Luther King and Gandhi. We are in awe of women like Harriet Tubman and Mother Teresa. But what does courage mean to us common folk? Where does the line get drawn between confidence and courage? Is there a rite of passage—a leap, if you will, that one makes into courageousness? As I prayed for insight in answering these questions, I knew that the answer would be universal, but a true separator of those who live rich, robust, deeply meaningful lives, and those who don't.

Courage is taking a deep breath and diving into an ocean looking for a treasure that you might not find. Not only is the probability of finding the treasure low, you may very well lose everything in the process. Nelson Mandela said that, "I learned that courage is not the absence of fear, but the triumph over it. The brave man is not he who does not feel afraid, but he who conquers that fear." My definition of courage applies to all of us. *Courage is placing such a high value on your belief, vision, idea, or conviction that you are compelled to act and take a risk, even if failure is a strong probable outcome. Courage is a knowing that the thing you must do is the right thing to do, no matter the cost.* I believe courage connects us to our spirit and brings us closer to God in a way nothing else can; we are totally dependent upon spirit for success. It is an all-in faith journey.

In coaching people over the years, I can tell the difference between those who are just confident and those who have moved to a higher level and have integrated courage in their lives. Courageous people have sacrificed. They know that they are not perfect. They have experienced fear and the possibility of defeat. They intuitively understand a weird paradox: risking it all creates a vulnerability that empowers us. These people have a greater sense of peace and authenticity. They seem to have a strong, non-pretentious self-comfort. There is something extremely humbling about being courageous because you are stripped naked before God and man. Courage exposes your vulnerability potentially for all to see. You have nowhere to turn but to you and your higher power. Courage sloughs away all of the pretenses and leaves you more purified. Of course, these are my musings, but I don't know that I've known a courageous person who didn't come very close to quitting or letting fear overtake them at some point in the process. This is very true the first time you embrace courage. There is a great, life-giving power in crossing over into courage that is unexplainable to those who have not walked the path. Frederick Douglass' life is a playbook on courage, but it all started when Douglass, at sixteen, physically challenged his master, who was known as a "slave breaker." His master never beat him after that, and Douglass started to plot his escape from slavery. Douglass went on to impact the world as an abolitionist and an advocate for women's suffrage and any other human injustice that he felt he could help right.

Acts of courage come in small forms every day. I submit that these small acts of courage have a cumulative, aggregate effect that shapes our world and emboldens us. People like the single mother who is determined to save her children from poverty by learning a trade or going to college. Or, the ex-convict who finds a better way to live, or the country girl who knows that getting her education is her ticket to more. Even the co-worker who stands up to a bully boss, knowing that she could lose her job. All of these seemingly small acts of courage rarely make headlines, but they do change lives every day. We love hearing about "real" heroes, and there are countless movies that we flock to that show us seemingly ordinary people accomplishing extraordinary feats. I'd like for you to take a moment to consider that the real hero is on the inside of you; you've just not gotten acquainted with him or her yet. What

act of courage do you need to take to reclaim or discover your joy, your peace, your life?

VALIDATION—TESTING

Validation is at the top of the transformation wheel.
Although it comes after courage, validation is the con-
tinuation of courage. It is the phase in the process where
you validate that your effort, energy, and perseverance
were worth the risks you took. This is the phase where
you dig deeper and you continue to test your act of
courage and leverage the learning and the internal fortitude that you've gained. Your eyes are opened about
yourself and what you value. Frederick Douglass was
a great writer only because he believed that education
was the key to freedom for every person, and certainly
every slave. In the beginning of his life, he had only
bits and pieces of learning. As a slave, he was forbid-
den to learn to read and write, but he secretly continued to learn as much as he could. Essentially, he taught
himself to read and write. His first book, *Narrative of*

the Life of Frederick Douglass, an American Slave, became a bestseller, and it was influential in promoting the cause of abolition.

Validation has its own energy and feel; it's laced with excitement and newness of mind and cause. It becomes the foundation from which you will continue to add to your life narrative both small and large acts of courage. Even if you fail along the way, the failure will educate you and strengthen you for the continued journey.

RESILIENCY — THE INTEGRATION OF BELIEF & FAITH

Our final stop on the wheel is resiliency. Resiliency is the integration process. All of your efforts, starting with self-discovery, then awareness, then confidence, then to courage, and on to validation, lead to this point. Resiliency is the recipe that makes you your authentic self. Earlier, we talked about authenticity. When we are intentional about living, we add layer upon layer of experience and wisdom to our life. We add those layers through the risks we are willing to take and the learning we are willing to embrace. Life will present opportunities for you to grow and go. It is up to you to decide whether it is worth the effort or not.

Fear is a BIG player for all of us, but it is also the equalizer. All of us have experienced fear to varying degrees and at varying levels. Resiliency eliminates our previous fears and replaces it with a new power that is an ever-present part of your new self. This fight that you've fought strengthens your knowledge about yourself and the world; this is your new normal. You've transformed yourself and your life in ways beyond what you imagined. You have a new understanding of your capacity, and you have more faith in who you are created to be. You are closer to understanding your purpose, your calling, and your potential. Then you go back to center, or should I say, you become more centered and move back to self-discovery. This new enlightened self seeks to know more, grow more, and be more. You will take many turns around the "Transformation Wheel" in a lifetime. It is not a one-trip wonder.

Remember the layers of the onion. With each layer, there is strength and added protection. The true shape takes form, and we can become proud of who we are and how we are connected to our Creator's design for our lives. When you transform every area of your life, there is very little room for toxic emotions and pettiness. You are too busy living and impacting the world to clutter your mind and spirit with negativity. Resiliency confirms that what you have decided to transform in your life is right. Your decisions contribute to your wholeness, your peace, and your power. This is the place where you believe that your life and the life of others will be richer because you made the choice. What choices do you need to make? What risks do you need to take?

6

THE POWER OF YOUR ASSIGNMENT: YOUR CALLING, GIFTS, AND TALENTS

I WAS TALKING TO A FRIEND ABOUT SOME OF her current professional challenges and opportunities. She was in her forties, and she made the comment that it has taken her well over forty years to grow up. I told her to not be so hard on herself because it actually takes a lifetime to "grow up." Growing up is ongoing. That's why understanding the Transformation Wheel discussed in Chapter 5 is so important. We really don't stop changing. Whether it's our bodies, our minds, or our spirits, we all are experiencing some type of evolution. Many of us try to be intentional about what that evolution looks like, and some of us are simply clueless and are not engaged in our life's journey at all.

I've never been musically inclined, but I've always had an appreciation for music, and I used to love to dance. When you're dancing, you are looking for the right beat to guide your movement. Once you figure that beat out, you fall into a rhythm that allows you to flow effortlessly through the entire song. Finding your assignment is very similar. Your call or assignment gives your life an energetic rhythm that allows you to flow effortlessly through each day with a sense of purpose and power. Finding that right rhythm is the key.

For the purpose of this book, we'll use the terms calling and assignment interchangeably. What do those terms mean? Your calling is your talent mixed with your energy to produce a positive reciprocating effect on your life and the lives of others. The mixture of your gifts, talents, and energy produces something that the world has never experienced before. Your unique mixture, when focused, can solve problems in the world like nobody else has before you. Your calling is both daunting and exhilarating at the same time. To know that there is a place for you in the world that no one else can fill gives you a sense of place and purpose. This one thought alone can change how we see ourselves and can impact the life decisions we make.

A large percentage of people in America are dissatisfied with their work. Studies show that 70% of people essentially hate their jobs. This is a very sad commentary. Your calling may or may not be the same as the work that you do to earn a living; however, understanding and embracing your calling makes any work you do a thousand times better. It helps you understand the value you bring to any organization or any situation. Your assignment extends far beyond what you earn in the marketplace. However, when you understand your calling/assignment, you are much more discerning in selecting jobs that are a better fit for your natural gifts and talents and what you value. I work with corporations on improving their culture. Sometimes people are unhappy, not so much because of the work itself, but because the culture and the environment they work in don't align with who they are. In cases where there is a disconnection in the culture, the person should seek another job. Just make sure you thoroughly research the culture of the new organization before jumping ship. As my grandmother used to say, you don't want to swap the witch for the devil! My very first job was with an outstanding company. I was able to grow and have opportunities; however, the work really didn't align with the type of work I wanted to do. It took me a while to figure that out, but I was misaligned because of the type of work, not the culture of the company. Either way, when you are misaligned, you need to do some soul searching. A large part of your life is spent working, so you need to make the best of it. When you are in a career that is a natural fit for you, your chances of excelling and adding value are much greater.

Walking in your calling allows your outlook on life to be much more positive and exploratory. Your emotional state is healthier, and you have very little time or mental space for toxicity. Your focus is better, and you are less likely to be self-absorbed and narcissistic in your thought patterns. "Reframing" your outlook really heightens your excitement about life in general.

It triggers your imagination to create and problem solve on a higher level, and this positive energy spills over into every area of your life. We all come here with gifts and talents that can be used for a greater purpose. Discovering what those gifts and talents are, throughout our lifetime, leads us to understand how those gifts should be used. Our calling is born from that knowledge. What makes us even more unique is that we are reared in different generations in different households with different values and perspectives. All of this adds another ingredient that shapes and molds us. Some of us may have the same gifts, talents, and even similar personalities, but because our backgrounds and upbringing are different, we'll approach the same issue in a different way. Those different approaches give our world richness of thought and creativity.

The million-dollar question is how does one identify his or her calling? There is no easy answer except that you must first seek to know what your calling is. Every individual must have a curiosity about their particular existence. Why do I exist? Why do I like this or that? That curiosity becomes like a magnet that draws you closer to discovering your calling. That curiosity compels you to try things that you are afraid of, but actually get a secret joy from doing. Uncovering your calling is a process of discovery. Your gifts and talents are like bread crumbs left on a trail. They can lead you to your calling, but your gifts and talents cannot stand alone on their own. They have to be connected to something greater. If you are a fantastic singer, to sing all day and all night for no good reason would bore you and eventually bore your audience. What is that singing connected to? What does it do for the world? You may find out that singing is simply a platform that allows you to have influence in areas that you are passionate about. Your calling is not a simple checklist. It's bigger than your gifts and talents; it is your connection to the divine.

GETTING STARTED: THE THREE STEPS

There are three key steps that will bring you closer to discovering your assignment. I like the word "assign-

ment" as much as I do "calling." The word "assignment" implies that there is work involved. Discovering
your assignment will require work. Once you discover
your calling, it will present an opportunity for a lifetime of joyous, fulfilling work.

The first step is easy. It simply requires you to think
about your childhood. When we are children, we
are more instinctive. Our minds are not as cluttered.
What were the things you enjoyed doing as a child?
For example, would you take things apart? Did you
always want a new pet? Were you trying to help your
friends with their homework? Did you play all manner
of instruments? Were you fascinated by history or art?
Did you enjoy taking care of your siblings and helping
your parents? Did you have a side-hustle as a kid?

I have very fond memories of spending quiet, quality
time with my grandparents, great aunts, and any adult
who seemed to know something important. I would ask
them tons of questions about God. I did play with other
kids, but I was never really a "kid" person. I had friends
growing up, but what I enjoyed more was reading fairy
tales, playing with dolls, and watching science fiction.

The original Star Trek was one of my favorites. I loved using my imagination. I had a desire to know the truth about myself and about life—I still do. I still read, not fairy tales, but I love fiction because it allows my imagination to wander. I still seek wisdom nearly every day. Whether I seek it from a podcast, mentors, or from God, I'm still asking questions that will improve my life and the lives of those I encounter on this journey. It may take you a while to identify the things that you were drawn to as a child, but start there. Write those special thoughts down; they will likely make you smile. Ponder them for a few days and see what emerges from your psyche. Feel free to ask people who knew you as a child what they remember about you and what you enjoyed doing. Your parents or close friends or perhaps teachers may give you some insight.

Many of us did not have a Disney World childhood. I heard someone say that we develop unhealthy coping skills in our childhood, and we spend all of our adult life trying to unpack and understand them. Don't dwell on your negative childhood experiences just yet. They have their place in shaping you. But, for this exercise,

I want you to think about the things you did when you played, activities you did well, and what you dreamed about doing. Think about where your mind would wander to in the quiet.

This first action puts your mind and spirit on alert that you are seeking to know more about yourself. The mind and spirit will then ready themselves and await your direction. They will be on the lookout for more information and insights because they know that you are ready for the journey.

Your first step dealt with your past, your childhood. Your second step requires you to examine your present. Start paying attention to what people ask you to do— both in your personal life and your work life. What is it that people are always asking you to participate in or help them with? This is a hint as to what you are good at because people will request you to do things that they believe you are capable of doing well. Interestingly enough, we often discern our talents through others. To us, our gifts are just "normal." We don't even recognize our gifts as gifts at all. Therefore, we don't put too much stock in those gifts being special or useful.

I coached a very talented leader who, in our third session, told me that he spoke five languages. He didn't see it as a big deal! Not only did he speak five languages, it was relatively easy for him to learn a new language. Let's just say we had a real in-depth conversation about that gift, which led to him doing some soul searching about his next career move. Initially, my coachee did not see his gift as special until I pointed it out to him. More often than not, others recognize our gifts before we do. What gift or talents do you have that you see as just "no big deal"? You have much to learn about yourself.

Thirdly, think about all of your activities during the day. Which of those activities energize you and make you smile? Cause you to forget about time and money? Then think about the things that drain you. Start making a mental list of the activities that energize you and the activities that drain you. Eventually, you need to write these two lists down. You'll need to also determine how much time you spend on each. If you spend the majority of your waking hours doing things that drain you mentally and spiritually, you're probably not operating in your giftedness. If nothing energizes you or brings you joy, it's past time for you to make some changes in your life! By the way, just because you have the skill set to do a particular task or job does not mean you are gifted in that area. I'm a skilled cook, but I don't like cooking. Planning and cooking for a dinner party drains and stresses me out! Because of my organized, strategic mind, which is one of my gifts, I can do it, but that doesn't mean that I should do it on a regular basis. And, I should certainly never have a career as a chef or an event planner! Your capacity to flourish and gain mastery in areas outside of your natural wiring is limited. Those learned skills should be seen as compliment to your natural gifts and talents; they are poor substitutes for your real gifts and talents. Tip: Don't write, "I love being with my kids and family," as one of the things that energizes you. Dig deeper. In theory, we should all enjoy being with our friends and family. Look at yourself as an individual. This is an opportunity for you to reflect and be a student of you.

These three activities will get you started: (1) Reviewing your childhood, (2) Talking to people who knew you as a child as well as people who know you now, and (3) Identifying what energizes you and what drains you. Keep a daily journal for at least a month or more on the activities that energize you and the ones that drain you.

These first three activities will start the conversation in your head about your calling; however, it doesn't end there. You have to ask yourself questions during the process. Most of these questions will be opened-ended and start with "why" or "how." *Why do I enjoy this? How does it connect to my past? My future? Why does this drain me? I used to love it—didn't I?* The answers will evolve as you grow and mature in the discovery process. As I said earlier, it takes a lifetime to grow up. The "whys" are your drivers. Your "whys" lead you to your passion. The word "passion" has been over-used and has lost some of its luster. For most of us, it is difficult to grasp what it means.

Discovering your "why" helps you get up in the morning, and it keeps you energized throughout the day. Your "why" is linked to something that you did or did not receive during your formative years (birth to twenty). Or it is linked to a life changing experience. Your "why" is connected to your values and worldview. Let me give you my personal example. My dad is my greatest hero. He encouraged me and told me that I could achieve impossible dreams. Now, this is important for a little black girl growing up in rural Georgia. It's life changing. His encouragement and love were constant. When I grew up, I realized that not everyone received this level of encouragement and love from a parent—especially a father. Many, many children grow up without their father even being involved in their life. I thought it was natural to receive encouragement from a parent. Somewhere along the way, I subconsciously figured out that the world is filled with people who didn't receive encouragement and direction. Lack of encouragement and direction has a profound impact on how we walk out our adult life. It is often a differentiator between success (unleashing one's potential) and failure (not reaching one's potential). I grew up feeling special and capable; it angers me when people are marginalized for any reason. There is great power in knowing and accepting who you are on this earth. Everyone has a light that directs their destiny. The conundrum is that all of us need someone to help us walk the path. We are made for relationships and community.

Every year I try to take my parents on vacation as a way to honor and show them how much I love and appreciate them. Plus, it's just fun making memories and spending time with them as an adult. I always learn something that I didn't know about myself or our family on those trips. On one of the recent trips, my dad shared with me that his father, my grandpa, told him that he would never amount to anything. I loved my grandpa dearly. He died when I was three. I spent a lot of time with him and my grandmother in my early years. They were my primary babysitters. So when my dad told me this, I could barely speak; there was a lump in my throat. I had a flood of emotions. My dad was the only one of his five siblings to finish high school—against his father's will. They were poor, and everyone had to go to work when they were old enough. My grandmother was determined that one of her children would have a high school education. My grandpa didn't value education as much as he did work. My grandmother valued education more than work. This story explains why my dad has always showered my two brothers and me with so much encouragement. Before my grandpa died, he told my dad that he was proud of him. That meant the world to my dad and to me. My daddy finished high school. I finished high school and college. My brothers finished college. My grandmother's act of courage changed what her child, and his children, and his children's children would be able to accomplish for generations to come.

Passion is a combination of love and hate. It is a constant fire that fuels your emotions and your conviction around what you believe is valuable and important. Passion ignites and pushes our courage forward. Encouraging others to discover and live their best life is what I am passionate about. It is what I'm called to do. It started with what my dad gave me: hope, a strong sense of self, character, integrity, and a belief that I am made in God's image to do great work on earth. I believe that truth for myself and for every human being.

As I mentioned earlier, my primary gift is that of a teacher. My assignment as a teacher is to encourage and exhort others in such a way that they gain wisdom about how to live their best life, and to help embrace how special they are. Anything I teach will have that bent because of what I received from my dad. Even teaching college English, I was mainly concerned with teaching writing skills that could support a person's ability to share their ideas, so they could get a good start to their career and beyond. I realize that I am a particular and peculiar type of teacher, and I use my gift as a teacher in ways that will be different from the millions of teachers that have come before me. All of my values, upbringing, environment, race, culture, education, skills, etc. will make my teaching style different from the teacher sitting next to me. Not better, but different and with a different assignment. If you are a gifted entrepreneur, your approach to business may be entirely different than the person next to you. The entrepreneur next to you may be a social entrepreneur who is called to fight poverty and injustice. While you may have the same gifts and talents, your assignment and energy will be used in different ways. The world needs your difference.

Your call is a lifetime adventure. It is a robust, never-boring way to live your life. There is always something for you to do and be a part of, regardless of your age. Your call has a universal value. In other words, you can live anywhere on earth and still there will be a place for your gifts and talents. Start with the three simple steps that I mentioned. You'll be amazed at what you discover about yourself once you start this process. You'll discover the rhythm of your life. You'll discover that your assignment serves both a spirtiual and a practical purpose. It connects you to your Creator and allows you to do meaningful, needed work that impacts humanity.

7

CAREER VERSUS CALLING: DEBUNKING THE MYTH OF THE PERFECT JOB

LL OF US WOULD LIKE TO HAVE A career that aligns with our calling. While it is certainly possible to have a career or a job that is perfectly matched to your calling, it's not necessary. Nor, is it possible for every person to have a job that aligns perfectly with what you believe your purpose is. Your call is broader and much bigger than your career. Your purpose is your spiritual core and is not limited to just one career or job. If that were the case, then your calling or purpose would be null and void when you retired from that particular job. Or, if you were terminated or laid off, you would cease to have a purpose. A calling stretches beyond the external circumstances and environment of the present day. It elevates you spiritually and impacts others in tangible ways.

THE PERFECT JOB MYTH

Some people spend their whole life looking for the perfect job or career path. The reality is that if you spent as much time discovering your calling, the perfect job or career path would appear. Too many of us spend a tremendous amount of energy trying to fit into a particular mold that we think others will find acceptable. Or worse yet, we chase money. Most find that at the end of the pot of gold is truly just a pot of gold. That pot of gold has no real intrinsic value. It can feed your gut, but not your soul. Spending time discovering your gifts, talents, and developing your skills will help you more clearly discern which career choice suits you. Your natural wiring (gifts/talents) will guide you towards meaningful work that energizes you. Most of us could have several different types of careers and be happy and fulfilled in those career choices. I love to solve difficult problems and develop strategies. I enjoy building things and bringing order and structure to chaos. I also like variety in my work because I'm easily bored. With my gifts and skill sets, there are several other career choices that I could have enjoyed as much as I enjoy my current work. I could have easily been a builder or real estate developer. Either of those careers would feed my creativity and my need to build something valuable and lasting. My career as a consultant allows me to build strong corporate cultures and help develop leaders. I am profoundly fullfilled and grateful for the work I get to do everyday.

If you understand your gifts and how to apply them, you can overlay your natural wiring and your calling on almost any job that you have. The interesting thing is once you understand your gifts, and are confident in your calling, you are not as fearful about new opportunities because you have a strong sense of how you can add value to any situation. If that new opportunity is a new job, promotion, or a community service project, you'll have clarity about what you bring to the table, so the work won't seem as daunting to you. Of course, in everything, there is a learning curve, and you'll be responsible for digging in and learning the process and the details of the work. But, you'll have a strong sense of how you can be effective, and your learning curve won't be as overwhelming because you'll have self-awareness about your strengths. You'll also have faith that you'll get "there" eventually. I used to get a little terrified when I was asked to serve on a board or to take on a new responsibility. Now, I rarely have that level of fear because I'm well versed on how I add value. Conversely, I'm also clear about the things I should steer clear of, so I don't get in over my head or become frustrated. I'm clearer about what I should say "yes" to and, more importantly, what I should say "no" to.

When you use your calling combined with a strong work ethic, you will be more effective, and you will enjoy whatever career or job you have. Many, many people are miserable in their jobs because they've not

made a clear connection to the work they are naturally wired to do. People are working in jobs that they
shouldn't be; therefore, they are drained at the end of
the day because it took all of their energy to do the
work that they weren't suited for or didn't like. For
example, an accountant who hates details and numbers
is going to struggle her entire career. Not only will she
struggle, she won't be a very good accountant. Your
gifts, talents, and skills are a part of your calling in
that they support your ability to walk in your call, but
you have a natural bent towards certain types of work
based on your innate abilities, personality, or physical
makeup. You may be six foot, eight inches, kinestheti-
cally inclined, and have terrific athletic abilities which
all may lead you to having a successful career in the
NBA. However, that career may energize you because
you are wired for it, but your call could be completely
different. Your call is an outward focus, while your gifts
and talents are more self-focused and inward.

Your "call" propels you towards a unique cause that
impacts the lives of other people. Your calling is neither
insulated nor isolated, but it has infinite impact that

reaches beyond you. Your calling is your legacy. It will be the things you do in abundance that will outlive you. Magic Johnson is a perfect example of someone whose career has afforded him the opportunity to help build strong communities in areas that are forgotten. He was a great NBA player who has become a highly success-ful entrepreneur with a purpose. His impact has been tremendous. He has evolved throughout his lifetime. My guess is that he has always cared about and under-stood the importance of community and entrepreneur-ship. Even if he had chosen another career path other than the NBA, at some point, he would have tried his hand at entrepreneurship and building better commu-nities. The scale may have been different, but the heart, the passion, and the call would have been the same.

We often see famous people, or people with a tre-mendous amount of wealth, end up living miserable lives. They have used their gifts and talents to build wealth or to achieve fame, but they never evolve beyond the wealth or the fame. Once they have the mansions, the cars, and the notoriety, there is nothing else that drives them, so they feel empty. This emptiness can lead to a downward spiral that is difficult to recover from. There was a study done on fifty ninety-year-olds. They were asked if they had to do life over again, what would they do differently. They said they would reflect more, take more risks, and do something that would outlive them. These are great words of wisdom. Reflection gives us permission to do real-time adjustments by self-examining our thoughts, our emotions, and our actions. Without regular reflection, we are less strategic about our life. Without risk, we limit our capacity to evolve. Without legacy living, we limit our impact on the world.

CAN YOUR CAREER AND CALL BE THE SAME?

Can your career and your call be the same? Absolutely! There are many people who have discovered that their career and call are one and the same. The greatest benefit of your career and call being the same is that you get to spend a tremendous amount of time and energy doing what you are called to do. An easy example would be that of a gifted school teacher. There are many teachers who are naturally wired to teach, and they feel that it is a calling on their life. They have a strong sense of the importance of the work that they do every day. Hopefully, all of us have had the experience of having one of these teachers during our school years.

Two of my high school teachers were phenomenal: Mr. Frederick Wright and Ms. Brenda Hudson. They had a tremendous influence on my love for literature, reading, and the English language. They brought beauty and magic to the classroom, and they challenged me to be the absolute best that I could. They didn't cut me any slack, so when this country girl from rural Georgia went to the university, I could not only compete, but excel. Ms. Hudson covered my essays in red ink. Mr. Wright made us recite Shakespeare and other notable authors every single day! They both, in their own way, pushed me past my fears and introduced me to my potential. Because of those two gifted teachers, I have a master's degree in English, and I have had the honor of teaching college level English. Mr. Wright and Ms.

Hudson were a tremendous influence in my life. Mr. Wright passed away many years ago, but the investment he made in my life still lives on in the people that I have taught and continue to teach. Never underestimate the impact your calling has to make the world and the people in it better.

MAKING THE DISTINCTION BETWEEN YOUR CAREER AND CALLING

It is important that you make the distinction between your career and your calling. They are not necessarily the same; however, they can and should work in tandem. Your career can certainly give you a platform or more influence in the area of your calling. My calling is to help people gain the wisdom they need to live an authentic and powerful life. My coaching and consulting work both give me daily opportunities to teach and guide people on how to live authentically and to walk in their power. As I mentioned earlier, even if I had a different career, such as a real estate developer, I would still seek and be drawn to opportunities to operate in my calling.

It is great if you can marry your calling and your career, but it's not necessary for you to live a fulfilled life. You could do volunteer work at your church or for a local non-profit that you are passionately engaged in, and that work connects you to your calling. The problem with most of us is that we allow our work to completely consume us to the point that everything else is edged out. There is very little substance or meaning in our daily lives. It's like being stuck in a revolving door where you keep pushing it around and around. Many people that I know enjoy their work, but they don't see it as their calling. I know of a maintenance supervisor who has been coaching little league baseball for many years. You could see his face light up when he talked about working with the kids. He is passionate about helping those kids because he wants them to have a positive role model in their lives. Having a positive role model was something he struggled with as a youth. This is his calling. He does a great job in maintenance, which is a job for which he is naturally wired because he is mechanically gifted, but that doesn't give him the same feeling of purpose as working with the little league teams.

However, in this same example, the maintenance supervisor could go back to college and get a degree in education and become a full-time baseball coach. In that case, he would be getting paid to do something that he feels called to do. While this would be great, it is not necessary unless that is what the person wants and has the energy, time, and resources to do. If you are sixty-three and close to retirement, going back to college may not be realistic, or it may be the perfect thing to do in the fourth quarter of your life. Either way, you can certainly find many opportunities to work with kids. As far as that is concerned, you could start your own non-profit with a few of your friends who are just as passionate as you are about working with youth. There are many ways to accomplish the same end.

If a person is a natural advocate for others, and they believe strongly in justice and fairness for all, they may be naturally wired to be an attorney. Well, in order to become an attorney, they will have to get an undergraduate and a law degree. Another person who does not have the degrees may be a natural advocate for others as well, but they may work in a trade as a union representative, or as a patient advocate in a hospital. All three of these people are doing work that they are naturally gifted in, but they do it in a different way and in different industries. Additionally, if all of these people are passionate about advocating for the rights of others, then they are also walking in their calling which just so happens to be a part of their job responsibilities.

Sometimes, we are lucky enough to stumble into work that is connected to our calling. You could discover on your current job that you have a knack for training other people. Whenever you train new employees, they are actually more successful, and turnover is not as high with the people you train. Although, training may be a small part of your daily responsibilities, it may be a job that you are better suited for in the long run, and a job that you should consider pursuing. Understanding your natural wiring and your call can give you a lot of insight and clarity when making career decisions. You'll also find yourself being much happier and more engaged in your daily work.

Work that you are naturally wired for will bring joy and a sense of mastery to your career choice. In 1983, Dr. Howard Gardner presented his theory around multiple intelligences. He theorized that only measuring an individual's I.Q. is short-sighted and limiting. According to Gardner, we have multiple intelligences that should be celebrated and leveraged. He gives us the following types: *intrapersonal (self-smart), interpersonal (people-smart), kinesthetic (body-smart), spatial-visual (picture-smart), linguistic (word-smart), logical-mathematical (number/reasoning smart), naturalist (nature-smart), and musical (music-smart)*. Take a look at this list. Which type of smart are you drawn to? Do you have great hand-eye coordination and are able to create and build with ease? Can you look at an empty space and "see" how it should be designed? Do people come to you constantly for advice and wisdom? You are a unique and complicated being—no surprise there. Figuring yourself out takes a lifetime. Have fun with the journey. Be thoughtful about what brings you joy, and what you do really well. What would you do for free? Or, what would you spend your time doing if you didn't have to work for money? Who would you help and why?

Seeking or creating work that you are called to do is a noble and worthy pursuit, but finding work that is the right fit for your talent is the starting point to success. Work that you are naturally wired for will require less energy, will improve your outcomes, and will ignite your creativity. Overall, you will be more valued in the marketplace, and you will be a much nicer person that the world will enjoy being around! At the end of the day, your calling and your career can be one and the same or completely different, and you can still experience the same joy of living a purposed life.

8

INTUITION: POWERFUL AND MAGICAL

WHAT IS INTUITION? IS IT SOME TYPE of mystical, elusive special power that only a certain finite group of people have? The answer is a resounding no. We all have intuitive powers, but we ignore them or do not acknowledge the value and practicality of this powerful tool. Intuition is a combination of instinct, experiences, and knowledge. Intuition is not rational thought, but it is our subconscious mind screaming at our rational mind. Albert Einstein said, "The **intuitive** mind is a sacred gift and the rational mind is a faithful servant. We have created a society that honors the servant and has forgotten the gift." Intuition is one of our highest and greatest forms of intellect; it informs rational thought. Knowing how to leverage your intuition sets you apart from everyone else. Our intuition creates both mastery and magic; it is where our internal artistry lives. It helps define and empower our uniqueness. When our gifts, talents, and calling are connected to our intuition we walk in the divine.

Animals have instinct, but their intellectual reasoning is limited. In the case of humans, instinct is that unexplainable, subconscious knowing that synchronizes with the conscious mind. The greatest leaders that I've had the honor of working with have a sixth sense about the work they do and what they are trying to accomplish. Many of them call it "their gut." I was sitting in a meeting with two C-suite executives and a couple of vice-presidents. I was reviewing my report on a dysfunctional work-group in their organization. As part of my report, I said that the manager of the work-group had minimal to no intuitive leadership ability. There was only one person in that room who understood what I meant by my statement. And he said, "Tangela, you actually have to practice intuition in order to have it." I smiled and said, "That is absolutely true." This CFO was one of the best in his struggling industry; he has since retired, but he is well-respected for what he accomplished in career. His connection to his "intuitiveness" has allowed that organization to thrive where many similar sized organizations have failed.

It is unlikely that you'll reach your peak performance if you do not embrace your intuitiveness. Intuition is what separates those who are average from those who are extraordinary. Connecting to your intuition means connecting to your innate magic. It's taking your gifts and talents to that magical "zone" where everything works like it's supposed to. Your confidence and zeal soar in that space. It is truly an exciting way to live. For the last several years, I have consistently practiced being more intuitive. It's been an exciting journey. While I certainly study my craft, I do not feel the need to "over prepare." I find that my accuracy and insight improve when I'm intuitive. So, in real-time, when I'm with my clients, I focus on listening with intent, being more open, and being present. I'm very good at synthesizing disparate information which allows me to connect dots that others may miss. Being present and open both allow me to recognize my clients' emotional and mental cues that they themselves may not notice. There have been countless times when a client has said, "How do you know that," or "I've never thought of it that way before," or "I've never made that connection." As a coach and consultant, I help people reconcile their thoughts and emotions, and challenge them to find a healthy, productive success strategy for their particular set of circumstances. This level of intuitive intensity is now my normal. It has taken my natural gift of discernment, teaching, etc. to an entirely different level. So much so, that I have to say, I would put my skill set up against anyone in the industry. That may sound arrogant, but my level of confidence has not come without work and a lot of self-discovery on my part. That confidence is also based on my results. When you truly operate in your calling, there will always be a positive response from others who have encountered or benefited from your calling. If you are a great artist, you'll touch the hearts of those who connect to your work. If you are a great cook, people will enjoy and desire your food. If you are a very organized and analytical person, people will seek you out to help them problem solve. The list goes on.

Warning!!!! Caution!!! Be sure you understand the following: You are only intuitive about things you are connected to or know something about. For example, you are never going to be intuitive about global warming if you've never studied it, have no interest in it—or worse yet—have no clue about the topic. Thus far, I have zero intuitiveness when it comes to singing or cooking. I'm tone deaf, and for some reason, I simply mess up recipes more often than not. I wouldn't dare trust my intuition when it comes to those two skills. They are not my gifts; I really don't understand how they even work. My subconscious mind has absolutely nothing valuable to work with in those instances. Don't try to manufacture intuition where it doesn't exist. It will not work for you.

Many of us, unfortunately, do try to manufacture gifts that are not ours, and we never really connect to our own innate abilities. When this happens, you get

people like the struggling singers who audition for the
television show "American Idol." These sincere, struggling singers can be very painful to watch. The same is
true on the stage of life when we try to be something
that we don't have the bandwidth, gifts, or talents to be.
It's the boss who really is not equipped to lead people,
but stays in his position for twenty years. He's miserable, and so is everyone else who works for him. He was
a great individual contributor, and someone thought
he could lead people. Whoops! Those are two different skill sets, talents if you will. After year two, he no
longer has the courage to make the right decision. His
performance gets worse as the years go by because he
feels desperate to keep his job and put on a good show.
Or, it's that pastor who really should be an evangelist
because he only has five good (really powerful) sermons
he can preach, and pastoring a flock really drives him
crazy. It's the person who is coaching little league baseball, but who can't stand to be around eight-year-olds.
How did that happen? From time to time, all of us will
enter the "twilight zone of confusion" while trying to

discover ourselves, but whatever you do, don't become a permanent resident of that craziness!

Intuition is so powerful that it will keep you from making a lot of stupid, non-productive mistakes. It will also be your guiding light towards making the right choices for your life. Acknowledging that your "gut" or intuition is a part of your higher ability to reason is the first step. Then, you have to practice using your intuition, so you can learn to trust and depend on it. When this happens, you will discover the magic of all that is you. Intuition brings it altogether and gives you a seemingly unnatural confidence in who you are and what abilities you have. You'll find that your outcomes are stronger, more valuable, and on target. Once I started to practice my intuitiveness in the areas of my giftedness, I started to see my abilities increase exponentially. Essentially, enlisting my intuition was the act of confirming my deep knowing through my experience and knowledge. When I would act upon that "sense," I found that I was right nearly 99.9% of the time. In order to operate at that level, you have to have a certain openness and know that there is no real "formula" that you can hang your hat on. Intuition is like a gasoline vapor. It's there. It's real. It can be measured, but you can't exactly put your hands on it. However, if someone decides to light a match, you'll definitely have some powerful activity happening.

It is true that intuition is somewhat messy and unde-fined. Especially, at first, when we try it out. But don't fret. There is a formula that I use that makes it less messy and less scary. If you've been reading so far, and you've identified through your own self-evaluations and the input of others as to what your gifts and talents may be, you're off to a great start. You can start to marry your intuition to that knowledge. Baby steps will be very helpful in laying the foundation. You can try it with very simple situations where the stakes aren't very high. It could be knowing what to say when talking to your boss. If you have a good idea that you would like to share with your boss, and you notice that she is dis-tracted or not in a good mood, then you might want to wait. If you ignore that warning sign, and plunge into the deep and the outcome is not what you expected, then whose fault is that? Yours or the boss? Whatever the case, take these baby steps. First, acknowledge that you will pay attention when you have an odd, unexplainable feeling. It can be a good or bad feeling that unexpectedly jumps into the middle of your psyche or thought process. The more you pay attention to these subconscious "highjackings," the more cognizant you will become of the role your intuition plays in your life on a daily basis.

Now that you are paying attention, you can move on to the next step, which is identifying why you feel a certain way. Ask yourself, what is my "gut" telling me about this situation or this circumstance. Intuition protects us from ourselves, others, and potentially dangerous situations. It evaluates our environment and the intentions of others. It prompts you to ask questions: What type of energy am I reading? Is it positive or negative? I once taught a brief portion of a sexual harassment class to a group of American foreign exchange students. The most important advice I gave them was to trust their intuition. I shared the story of what happened to me in my twenties. This was way before the "Me Too" movement. I had traveled for work and was staying at a hotel for a company conference. At about 9:30 p.m., my phone rang. It was a man who worked for the same company, but he was a manager in a different region. I had met him several times before, and he was always professional and cordial. However, that night, I was so startled by his call that I could barely talk in the beginning of the conversation. After a few minutes, I was able to regain my senses, and I asked him why he was calling. My question caught him by surprise. He said he thought I might need a mentor since I was new to the company. I told him thanks, but no thanks. I asked him how his then pregnant wife was doing, and told him to never contact me again unless it was strictly work related. I hung up the phone, and I was terrified. There was no Caller ID at that time, so I didn't know if he was downstairs or close by. Now, my situation was a bit extreme, but my intuition probably saved me from future problems. Although this man was careful not to make overt overtures on the phone, his tone indicated he was clearly moving in that direction. My brain kept screaming, "Why is he calling me so late while I'm at this hotel; he's not even supposed to be at this meeting! What is going on here?" Those were the two questions that I needed answered. This guy had no logical reason to call me despite what he said. When I asked him the questions, he became uncomfortable. It is also interesting to say that I later saw a friend of his who could not look me in the eye. I suspect he had something to do with "setting up" this little event. Both of these men were in management. From that moment forward, I put boundaries in place to make sure I was never in a compromising situation during my travels for work or otherwise. I also decided that I would call it like I saw it if anyone else tried that tactic on me. It has been well over twenty years since that happened, but I'm certain that man's intentions were not honorable. When I asked about his pregnant wife, he started to do some serious backpeddling. In order to use your intuition effectively, you have to define why you feel the way you feel. Sometimes that can be done in a couple of minutes, and sometimes it can take days or weeks. This is the process of validating and bringing all of your subconscious knowledge and experiences to the forefront, so you can objectively evaluate why you feel the way you feel. In my particular case, I was taught that the only people that call you late at night are close family and friends, and at a certain hour, it is disrespectful to call people unless it is an emergency. That social more was the first piece of data that my emotions and mind went to. I later surmised that there could be only one reason a married man would be calling a young inexperienced woman at a hotel late at night.

There have been so many times that my intuition has opened up opportunities for me in business. I've been able to discern who great clients were and clients that would be more challenging to assist. My intuition is a very close companion of mine. It helps guide my decision making and judgment. Sometimes it's the final decision maker, and other times it simply starts my research process. So practicing your intuition and defining the "why" of your gut feeling both move you towards trusting your intuition in conjunction with your other mental and spiritual faculties. It is important to understand that your intuition must be supported by some realm of objectivity. In other words, you have to plug your rational mind into the process. It's interesting to note that, generally speaking, women are more intuitive than men. A lot of that has to do with the fact that women have longer memories, and since our memories are connected to our experiences, we have to be careful to make sure that what we are feeling is valid. That "gut" feeling can be so distorted by past hurts and disappointments that we can't have sound judgment about a particular person or circumstance. Giving your "why" a name is key to properly using your intuition.

The formula is simply this: (1) Acknowledge your intuition, (2) Practice using your intuition, and (3) Give yourself time to name your "why." When coaching, I often ask clients to explain what their intuition is telling them—especially if they are trying to make a very difficult decision. I asked one manager about what his intuition was telling him about a person he was considering hiring. He said everything looked good on paper, and the person had a very good interview. He said they were extremely smart. I remember that he looked at me sort of weirdly when I asked him that question. Well, he hired the person, and he probably should have given his intuition a little more time to name his "why." That particular hire was a very long, painful, challenging experience for him. This person became very disruptive for his team. Needless to say, he and I talked a lot about intuition after that.

In my opinion, our intuition exists for four main reasons. (1) To warn us of impending danger (emotional or physical), (2) to help us improve our judgment, (3) to exponentially grow our talents, so that our calling is more powerful, and (4) to help us recognize good opportunities. On any given day, your intuition can be your best, most trusted friend who helps you grow and know in powerful, magical ways.

9

BE PRESENT . . . EVERY DAY.

OW OFTEN ARE YOU IN A CONVERSA-
tion with a friend, co-worker, or spouse and
you're really just waiting for them to shut
up, so you can get your important point across? You're
probably in those situations more than you care to
admit. You can be physically in a room with someone,
but not be present. And while we all have an intrinsic
need to be heard, often we scream when we should be
quiet, and we are quiet when we need to scream. Our
protocol for being present is broken, and therefore we
miss opportunities to explore and grow our potential.
We are simply not engaged in the moment we are in;

we push towards the future to escape the present. When the future arrives, half of the time, we don't even notice. We humans are funny creatures.

Every day holds its own treasure trove of hope and knowledge. That treasure has to be mined and discovered. Approaching every day as a treasure hunter, a daily seeker, will slow you down. You'll start to take notice of people and situations like never before. You'll quiet the noise in your head. Eventually, you'll be able to discern what is important to you, and what is not. What fills your tank, and what drains your energy? When this new day that has never existed before in history arrives, what will you do with it? What will you learn from it before it fades into eternity? Did you discover anything meaningful or useful? Or, was today a blur? Your opportunity lives in today not tomorrow. Today prepares you for tomorrow. Your ability to recognize that is key to living a robust, called life. Hopefully, you are better in some way than you were yesterday. The problem is that becoming better is nearly impossible if you simply treat Monday like Tuesday and Tuesday like Wednesday. You have to understand that last Monday is nothing like this Monday. Perhaps you are the same bored, lackluster person that you were last week, but the world is not. The world is vast. Millions of changes and developments have taken place without your knowledge and without your contribution and input. It wasn't because you couldn't, it was because you didn't value the moment you were in. You didn't pay attention to yourself, the signs all around you, nor did you learn from others. There was no application of knowledge, no new distribution of productive energy, no new thoughts, or new relationships. You simply put everything on autopilot, and decided, unconsciously, that was enough. You slowly unplugged from your energy source.

When we don't do a good job of respecting the day that we are in, the effect is cumulative. We wake up one day and ten, twenty, or more years have flown by. I've had the sad occasion to see what an immature, under-developed seventy-year-old looks like. It ain't pretty! Are you on that road? Can you pinpoint the last time you paid attention to your life and how you felt? Or, has life happened so fast that you didn't feel you could slow down long enough to grasp what was going on in your heart and mind? This chaos happens to all of us, but how long you stay in your dark, undefined tunnel is up to you.

I've had the pleasure of seeing several seventy and eighty-year-olds who still lead very powerful energetic lives; they also have a peace about them. A dear friend of mine, who has children who are much older than me, gave me some wisdom about aging that I've never forgotten. She said, "I am the same person with the same desires, same heart, and zest for life that I've always had. It's just that the body starts to wear down, but as long as I'm healthy, I'm fine." I don't think that I will ever forget her perspective. The exterior shell, the body, loses its durability, but the spirit and the mind should always fight to actively participate in living a robust, called life.

All of my mentors have been older than me. In most cases, they have been at least twenty years or more older than me. I've been amazed by their wisdom and purposed way of living. I've observed how they have contributed to the world, but also to me. The fire in their eyes is very vibrant. They have a generous spirit when they share their time, knowledge, and wisdom. I've always noticed how they are fully engaged when we talk. No cell phones, computers, etc. I have their undivided attention for the time we are together. I ALWAYS leave those meetings smarter and with more clarity about whatever we discussed, or the lesson they were teaching me. I'm so grateful that they built lives for themselves that spilled over and help direct my journey. I have learned that we need each other to be great; greatness is not usually formed in isolation, but it is meant to be shared.

ABUNDANCE VERSUS SCARCITY

As I mentioned, being fully present every day is important. Equally as important is having a generous, sharing spirit. There is something about each of us that makes us want to contribute to someone or something outside of ourselves, in a meaningful way. It could be visiting the nursing home, or reading to children at the library, or preparing a nice meal for someone whose child is very ill. Or, it could be as simple as complimenting someone on their work, or their shoes! We are elevated by the act of generosity, both when we act in a generous way and when kindness is extended to us. Generosity and goodwill connect us to our common humanity more than any other thing we do. It is universal.

Generosity has nothing to do with how wealthy you are; it has more to do with your mindset towards abundance. If you believe that the world is an abundant place which reciprocates and multiplies goodness, then you are more likely to extend your gifts, talents, and resources as a type of investment with a guaranteed great return. If you are a person who operates in scarcity, you will hold tight to all that you have, or think that you should have it all. Scarcity thinking is present in the very wealthy as well as those who are impoverished. This self-imposed, narrow mindset limits a person's growth. A scarcity mindset makes you less likely to connect with people or opportunities that may require you to invest time, energy, or resources. Scarcity says, "I don't have enough to spare." I have had people in my life who believe that they have to hold on to everything or it will slip away. There is one consistent thread that I've noticed: they have low, negative energy, and they seem to radiate little to no joy. Think about your day, your week, your month. Create two columns and title them "Generosity" and "Scarcity." Keep a journal of when you have given of your time, talent, and resources, and when you have acted in ways that are self-focused and selfish. What do your columns look like? Where might you need to make some changes? We are all selfish by nature until we are not. Once we discover the value of an abundant mindset, we become whole and fulfilled—purposed.

SELF-DISCIPLINE AS A SELF-STARTER

Discovering your call and ultimately operating in the center of your call will take some self-discipline. None of us like to hear that word; something about it seems like drudgery instead of fun. Despite how we feel about the word, it is the foundation for creating the right habits around our dreams, desires, and calling. There is no getting around it. I have been exercising for years, but I hate it! There is nothing about exercise that appeals to me. But, I love feeling strong and healthy, so I can do the work that I'm called to do. Your good habits will create a power in themselves, both mental and physically. They provide the skeletal suit for everything else. Our skeletal system props our bodies up, so our organs are protected and our muscles can function. Think about self-discipline as your skeletal suit for the body of work that you are called to do. Nothing can be accomplished without some level of discipline. We all require different amounts at different times. But make no mistake, the act of adding a dose of discipline is paramount. For years, at the beginning of each year, I would pray for personal development and growth in a certain area of my life—I still do. One year, I prayed really hard for self-discipline. Around the second quarter of the year, as I was re-praying this prayer, it was impressed upon me that it was useless to pray for something that I already am. In other words, I'm already a disciplined person, I just need to walk in discipline and stop talking . . . and oh yeah . . . praying about it. Well that was a self-starter for me, I have to say. I took that seriously. That particular revelation helped me write this book. You have to learn how to eat the elephant daily, that's why being present is so important. Being present will give you insight about how to prioritize your day. Most of us are reactionary and are driven by our tasks, versus having a strategy for what we want to accomplish. We live too much in the weeds not in the clouds. The clouds will give you a broader picture that can help you create a road map that drives your activities. Take some time at the beginning of the week to contemplate what you want to learn or accomplish during that particular week. What encounters do you need to have? Who do you need to talk to? What podcasts do you need to listen to? What tasks need to get done? When you focus in this way, the tasks are simply a part of a bigger picture. For example, my daughter needed to improve her grade in science, and she needed my help with studying and memorizing the periodic table. Well my "big picture" with my daughter during her pre-teen years was to spend time with her and make sure that the lines of communication are always open. It's intentional parenting. Helping her with her homework is one of the many tasks that add up to better communication and a wonderful relationship. If we focus a little more on "cloud thinking" the tasks will reveal themselves, and you will be able to select the tasks that give you the greatest return and outcomes.

CLOSING THOUGHTS, REFLECTIONS, DEDICATION

When I told my dad that I was writing this book, he smiled and said, "That's great because you have a lot to say that people need to hear." I almost cried at his words. He was right about me, but he was also right about all of us. As you read these words, you are writing your own narrative. Your story. I started by talking about my funeral, and how I want it to be short, not long and drawn out because my life should speak for itself. However, since I did watch most of Aretha Franklin's funeral, I've had to adjust my thinking a tiny bit. People celebrated her life for weeks. Her funeral lasted for several hours, but it was an awesome reflection of a life well-lived. I expect to live a well-lived life.

There is so much to say that it is impossible to write it all down without creating a *Moby Dick*-like epic. Much of what I've written requires action on your part. Your mind has to change, and that will take a while—believe me, I know! Real change happens when we have sustained focus over time. You've managed to create habits that are counterproductive to you living a called and a joyous life. It will take time and attention to rekindle the desire to live out your assignment. Getting on the right path is possible for all of us at any age. The sooner you get started, the more life you get to live.

If I were going to summarize this book in one paragraph it would go as follows: Life can hand us a ton of challenges, but those who pay attention to them can learn and grow from the struggles. Those who don't pay attention will likely never taste the joy of living. Living the purposed life is a process of discovery that never ends. There is a logic and rhythm to that type of living that eventually becomes intuitive. It is both spiritual and practical. Your life will be transformative for you and transformative for those you are connected to. There is a powerful energy that flows through people who take the risk of living a purposed (not perfect) life.

I dedicate this book to my amazing parents. They were ahead of their time. They poured into me all that they had to make sure I would have the tools needed to live life successfully. I honor their love and investment in me by paying it forward to the rest of the world.

I also dedicate this book to my aunt Shirley. Her untimely death forced me to explore my life. For that, there are no words. Perhaps, Paul of Tarsus said it best: *"And we know that all things work together for good to them that love God, to them who are the called according to his purpose."* Romans 8:28 King James Version

EPILOGUE

THE PURSUIT OF WHOLENESS:
SPIRIT, SOUL, AND BODY

Gaining mastery over self is both a full-time and life-time job. We all want to find that perfect balance of joy and peace that fills us with purpose and a sense of well-being. But sometimes it seems that once we get one part of our life going well, the other falls off track. We are complex and multifaceted creatures who evolve and grow based on our desire to know more about who our best self is. We are always pursuing the right balance and order to our lives, often subconsciously. The purpose of this book is to get you to pursue it consciously and daily. In order to do that, you have to know how you're built.

You are comprised of three parts: spirit, soul, and body. These three mesh together and form a being that has never been created before, nor will the earth see this special being again. This special person is you. Your body is your external shell, your physical self. It needs food, water, sunlight. It plays to the five senses: touch, sight, hearing, smell, and taste. It should be the least powerful of the three, but often it takes the lead and takes center stage in an unhealthy way. It becomes so powerful that many of us can't seem to resist a cupcake, or any source of an endorphin rush. It becomes more astute than our soul at getting us to do things that we need to resist.

Our soul is our mind, emotions, intellect, our ego, our personality. It is the part of you that makes you unique and different from everyone else. It is the control center for the rest of you. Yet, we don't seem to give it the respect or time it needs to properly guide us. Instead of being mindful, we are often mindless. Mindfulness has to be approached respectfully each day. Carving out time to make sure that our emotions are checked, and that we will use our intellect in a productive way, is a matter of choice. We also have our wonderful, or not so wonderful, personalities that we can control or let run amok.

We can guide our soul energy force in a way that allows us to refuse the third cupcake because our intellect tells us that an excessive amount of sugar spikes our insulin levels. Or, if we are eating the cupcake for emotional reasons, we can take the time to discover and resolve those issues, so we are better at self-care. This powerful control center reminds me of the bridge of the Star Trek Enterprise. It's a place where all of the exciting decisions are made that can drive you at warp speed into amazing new territories. Or, it can take you into a black hole. It really all depends on which buttons you push.

Neither your soul nor your body has anything on your spirit. It is the magical part of you that is unexplainable, but yet when allowed, it has a multiplier effect that is unstoppable. It supplies the soul with its will and determination to overcome, to build, and to conquer. Our spirit connects us to our creator so that we can rise beyond the natural and propel ourselves to a much higher calling and way of living.

I loved listening to the speaker and prolific author, Wayne Dyer. He was a spiritualist who studied other spiritualists and shared with people how they too could walk more in spirit. I was always fascinated by his determination and passionate commitment to share with people the beauty of knowing and understanding the spiritual side of themselves. Even those who identify as atheists have a spiritual side that may or may not go unacknowledged. Your belief or lack of belief in a higher power doesn't give you an automatic spiritual-ectomy. None of us can fully explain the energy attached with a certain person. When a person who has presence enters a room the atmosphere changes. It could be good or bad change. Or, when a new team member is added at work, dynamics change for better or worse. As individuals, we are connected to a type of energy that expands beyond the physical realm. We don't fully understand why we love our children so deeply, but we do. I shall never forget, after my daughter was born, I was lying in the hospital bed fully asleep, and in a moment, I was wide awake for no particular reason. I mean, I had just given birth a few hours earlier, so I was obviously exhausted! After being awake for about three minutes, the nurse walked in holding my daughter. She informed me that my daughter seemed to be hungry, and indeed she was. There was a connection to my newborn daughter that was unexplainable in the natural; it was indeed spiritual. It still is. My husband and I met on a blind date; we have been inseparable since our first date over two and half decades ago. He is still my very best friend. I cannot explain either of these instances in tangible ways; but, the impact that these two people have had on my life is everything. Both my mom and dad poured their love and wisdom into me in ways that shaped who I am today and what I have the capacity to become. It is inexplicable but for our spirit.

One of the greatest values of any religion is that it should connect you to your creator and your spiritual self. If your religion is just a matter of habit or tradition, its power is limited as to what it can do to help you live out your life. My Judeo-Christian faith connects me to my powerful God. His ability to empower me with

wisdom through His Holy Spirit produces an awesome-
ness in my life that is often overwhelming and beautiful all at the same time. I'm connected to Him and
His will for my life in a way that clarifies my purpose
and gives me a centered place that is a strong foundation from which to live. Of course, this is only true if I
stay rooted and connected to my heavenly Father. The
earthly realm, which is comprised of our bodies and
souls, wars against our spirit. Our spirit desires peace
more than anything, but our daily grind causes us to
either ignore or evade the complexity of connecting to
our spirit man.

My peace, joy, and love all are derived from His
grace. There is a spiritual continuity that is a stabiliz-
ing force and resides in the center of my being. Everything emanates from the core source of my spirit. I am
simultaneously powerful and peaceful in spite of the
external, so when the Uber driver said I had a "relaxed
power" my spirit leaped at that truth. I couldn't get the
words out of my head for days, for weeks. I thought,
"Did God send me to Phoenix, AZ to get two words?"
Perhaps, He did. He gave me language that defined

what I've been striving for and, ultimately, what I want others to know and embrace. Everyone should experience what it's like to have a relaxed power that allows you to live a purposed (not perfect) life. What more can you ask for?

For some of you, this all sounds very spooky and strange. That is totally understandable. For others, you're saying, "I get it, but how do I get there? How do I contact and connect with my spirit?" Connecting with your spirit is found in the quiet places. I have a quiet room in my home. The neutral colors and the windows both have a calming effect on me. If you have ever been to the beach, in the midst of listening to the waves crashing and seeing the beautiful colors, you find that your blood pressure goes down almost instantly. That feeling of being on the beach transitions your energy to a more quiet, reflective space. A space where there is no noise—only you, your thoughts, and your prayers. First, integrate quiet time in your life. Time that doesn't include electronic devices. Some of you are true extroverts, so quietness makes you uncomfortable, but everyone has to be quiet in order to listen.

Some of you can find this time while exercising or going for a jog. The quiet gives you a new time to observe all things in your environment, and to gauge whether they are energizing you or distracting you from a closer connection to your purpose, your power, and your peace. I always pray for wisdom, and I expect wisdom to show up when I pray. It always does. The timing may take longer than I want, but the wait expands my patience, which is something I'm in constant need of. Wisdom is one of God's promises to me. His promise is that he will not withhold wisdom from those who ask (James 1:5). Observation of creation and people also connect you with spirit. You start to see the miraculous and the unexplainable artistry of the creator, which heightens your reverence and appreciation for a greater power. I shall never forget the first time I went to the Grand Canyon. I stood there in awe and started to weep. I had not anticipated such an emotional reaction to this natural wonder, but something about the entire experience took my breath away. It gave me a view of my scale—my smallness in juxtaposition to His greatness, but I also perceived my significance and part of the whole of mankind.

Grappling with the three parts of you is a constant juggling act. If you have ever seen a juggler get started, he really throws up one ball at a time, and eventually he gets them all going. Once they are going, it looks effortless. This effortlessness comes from practice and determination. Your Spirit, soul, and body are like those balls. It takes work and effort to keep them all in the air at the same time. Even if you drop one from time to time, it's okay. Just pick it up and start again. His mercies are new each and every day. Your power and peace come from you respecting and valuing your divine nature.

All My Best,

Tangela

PRAYER OF POWER
BY TANGELA W. JOHNSON

Dear Heavenly Father, help us to be present in this very moment, so that we can gain the insights we need to be great in every aspect of our lives. We are mothers, fathers, sisters, daughters, brothers, sons, employees . . . and at times, we are overwhelmed and exhausted by the roles and responsibilities we shoulder. Help us to understand that we cannot do your job and be God to or for people. Give us peace and a true understanding of what is really important on this short journey called life. Give us the courage to say yes to that which is connected to our purpose and no to the things that distract and drain us. Help us be good stewards of our time, our resources, and our emotional energy.

We pray for and respectfully ignore those who have tried to box us in and label us. We understand that it is you, the Creator of the Universe, who before the foundation of the world, molded us and set our path. Help us to understand that anything that keeps us from successfully fulfilling our purpose is either a falsehood or a bad memory. You created us to be bold, to be powerful and to be purposed. Our gifts and talents make room for us on this earth. We are not driven by our ego; we understand that humility is not thinking less of ourselves, but instead it is thinking of ourselves less. We are strong in you. No weapon formed against us shall ever prosper. We are mighty enough to extend grace and mercy to those who have hurt us. We stand in solidarity in putting those things in the past behind us and pressing forward towards the higher call. We understand that all things are possible with you. You have given us the faith and the tools to manifest our destiny. Without question, we embrace the fact that you will do exceedingly, abundantly above all that we can ask or imagine. It is in that spirit, that we remove our small thinking of who we are and seek to discover our greatness. Father, let us be like Deborah, the Judge of the Old Testament, not daunted by our fears, but determined warriors filled with wisdom and the revelation of our true selves.

Let our bodies be nourished and strengthened. Let the fellowship of like-minded-ness feed our soul, and let our spirit soar on eagle's wings. Father, in your Holy Name, and in the name of your Son, we receive these great blessings from you and count them as already done.

AMEN

CPSIA information can be obtained
at www.ICGtesting.com
Printed in the USA
BVHW042138230922
647911BV00003B/60

9 781734 234626